WORLD
HISTORY SERIES

The Bombing
of Pearl Harbor

Titles in the World History Series

The Age of Augustus
The Age of Exploration
The Age of Feudalism
The Age of Napoleon
The Alamo
America in the 1960s
The American Revolution
Ancient Chinese Dynasties
Ancient Greece
The Ancient Near East
Aztec Civilization
The Battle of the
  Little Bighorn
The Black Death
The Bombing of Pearl Harbor
The Byzantine Empire
Caesar's Conquest of Gaul
The California Gold Rush
The Chinese Cultural
  Revolution
The Civil Rights Movement
The Collapse of the
  Roman Republic
Colonial America
The Conquest of Mexico
The Constitution and the Founding of
  America
The Crash of 1929
The Crimean War
The Crusades
The Cuban Missile Crisis
The Early Middle Ages
Egypt of the Pharaohs
Elizabethan England
The Enlightenment
The French Revolution
Greek and Roman Mythology
Greek and Roman Science
Greek and Roman Sport
Greek and Roman Theater

The History of Rock & Roll
The History of Slavery
Hitler's Reich
The Inca Empire
The Industrial Revolution
The Inquisition
The Italian Renaissance
The Korean War
The Late Middle Ages
The Louisiana Purchase
The Making of the Atom Bomb
Mayan Civilization
The Mexican-American War
The Mexican Revolution
The Mexican War of
  Independence
Modern Japan
The Mongol Empire
The Persian Empire
Pirates
Prohibition
The Punic Wars
The Reagan Years
The Reformation
The Renaissance
The Rise and Fall of the
  Soviet Union
The Rise of Christianity
The Roaring Twenties
Roosevelt and the New Deal
Russia of the Tsars
The Salem Witch Trials
The Stone Age
The Titanic
Traditional Africa
Twentieth Century Science
Victorian England
The War of 1812
Westward Expansion

WORLD
HISTORY SERIES ▪▪▪

The Bombing of Pearl Harbor

by
Earle Rice Jr.

Lucent Books, P.O. Box 289011, San Diego, CA 92198-9011

Library of Congress Cataloging-in-Publication Data
Rice, Earle, Jr.

   The Bombing of Pearl Harbor / by Earle Rice Jr.
      p.   cm.—(World history series)
   Includes bibliographical references and index.
   Summary: Discusses the people and events involved in
Japan's decision to attack Pearl Harbor, which forced the
United States to enter World War II.
   ISBN 1-56006-652-0 (alk. paper)
   1. Pearl Harbor (Hawaii), Attack on, 1941—Juvenile litera-
ture. [1. Pearl Harbor (Hawaii) Attack on, 1941. 2. World War,
1939–1945—Causes. 3. Japan—Foreign relations—United States.
4. United States—Foreign relations—Japan.] I. Title. II. Series.
D767.92 .R54 2001
940.54'26—dc21   99-050970

Copyright 2001 by Lucent Books, Inc., P.O. Box 289011,
San Diego, California 92198-9011

Printed in the U.S.A.

Contents

Foreword

Each year on the first day of school, nearly every history teacher faces the task of explaining why his or her students should study history. One logical answer to this question is that exploring what happened in our past explains how the things we often take for granted—our customs, ideas, and institutions—came to be. As statesman and historian Winston Churchill put it, "Every nation or group of nations has its own tale to tell. Knowledge of the trials and struggles is necessary to all who would comprehend the problems, perils, challenges, and opportunities which confront us today." Thus, a study of history puts modern ideas and institutions in perspective. For example, though the founders of the United States were talented and creative thinkers, they clearly did not invent the concept of democracy. Instead, they adapted some democratic ideas that had originated in ancient Greece and with which the Romans, the British, and others had experimented. An exploration of these cultures, then, reveals their very real connection to us through institutions that continue to shape our daily lives.

Another reason often given for studying history is the idea that lessons exist in the past from which contemporary societies can benefit and learn. This idea, although controversial, has always been an intriguing one for historians. Those who agree that society can benefit from the past often quote philosopher George Santayana's famous statement, "Those who cannot remember the past are condemned to repeat it." Historians who subscribe to Santayana's philosophy believe that, for example, studying the events that led up to the major world wars or other significant historical events would allow society to chart a different and more favorable course in the future.

Just as difficult as convincing students to realize the importance of studying history is the search for useful and interesting supplementary materials that present historical events in a context that can be easily understood. The volumes in Lucent Books' World History Series attempt to present a broad, balanced, and penetrating view of the march of history. Ancient Egypt's important wars and rulers, for example, are presented against the rich and colorful backdrop of Egyptian religious, social, and cultural developments. The series engages the reader by enhancing historical events with these cultural contexts. For example, in *Ancient Greece*, the text covers the role of women in that society. Slavery is discussed in *The Roman Empire*, as well as how slaves earned their freedom. The numerous and varied aspects of every-day life in these and other societies are explored in each volume of the series. Additionally, the series covers the major political, cultural, and philosophical ideas as the torch of civilization is passed from ancient Mesopotamia and Egypt, through Greece, Rome, Medieval Europe, and other world cultures, to the modern day.

The material in the series is formatted in a thorough, precise, and organized manner. Each volume offers the reader a comprehensive and clearly written overview of an important historical event or period. The topic under discussion is placed in a broad, historical context. For example, The Italian Renaissance begins with a discussion of the High Middle Ages and the loss of central control that allowed certain Italian cities to develop artistically. The book ends by looking forward to the Reformation and interpreting the societal changes that grew out of the Renaissance. Thus, students are not only involved in an historical era, but also enveloped by the events leading up to that era and the events following it.

One important and unique feature in the World History Series is the primary and secondary source quotations that richly supplement each volume. These quotes are useful in a number of ways. First, they allow students access to sources they would not normally be exposed to because of the difficulty and obscurity of the original source. The quotations range from interesting anecdotes to farsighted cultural perspectives and are drawn from historical witnesses both past and present. Second, the quotes demonstrate how and where historians themselves derive their information on the past as they strive to reach a consensus on historical events. Lastly, all of the quotes are footnoted, familiarizing students with the citation process and allowing them to verify quotes and/or look up the original source if the quote piques their interest.

Finally, the books in the World History Series provide a detailed launching point for further research. Each book contains a bibliography specifically geared toward student research. A second, annotated bibliography introduces students to all the sources the author consulted when compiling the book. A chronology of important dates gives students an overview, at a glance, of the topic covered. Where applicable, a glossary of terms is included.

In short, the series is designed not only to acquaint readers with the basics of history, but also to make them aware that their lives are a part of an ongoing human saga. Perhaps they will then come to the same realization as famed historian Arnold Toynbee. In his monumental work, A Study of History, he wrote about becoming aware of history flowing through him in a mighty current, and of his own life "welling like a wave in the flow of this vast tide."

IMPORTANT DATES IN THE HISTORY OF THE BOMBING OF PEARL HARBOR

January. Admiral Isoroku Yamamoto, commander in chief of the Combined (Japanese) Fleet, initiates a study for a surprise attack on Pearl Harbor.

April 10. The Imperial Japanese Navy establishes the First Air Fleet (*Kido Butai*) commanded by Vice Admiral Chuichi Nagumo.

November 5. Admiral Yamamoto issues Operation Order No. 1, which establishes December 7, 1941, as the date of the Pearl Harbor attack (X day for Operation Hawaii); Tokyo notifies Ambassador Nomura of the November 25 deadline on negotiations.

September 6. Japan decides to go to war with the United States "when necessary."

November 3. Ambassador Joseph C. Grew warns Washington of potential surprise attack by Japan.

November 7. Ambassador Nomura presents Proposal A, a program continuing diplomatic dialogue with the United States, to Secretary Hull.

January 1941	April	October	November

March. Commander Minoru Genda completes first draft of a plan to attack Pearl Harbor.

April 16. Secretary of State Cordell Hull issues the Four Principles for resolving differences between the United States and Japan.

October 18. The Japanese general staff accepts Admiral Yamamoto's plan to attack Pearl Harbor (under threat of his resignation).

November 17. Japanese officer pilots receive final briefing aboard *Akagi.* Ambassador Grew again warns Washington of a possible Japanese surprise attack.

November 19. Tokyo dispatches "Winds" instructions to its Washington embassy.

November 22. Tokyo extends negotiations deadline until November 29.

November 24. Hull meets with representatives of Great Britain, China, Australia, and the Netherlands to discuss Roosevelt's compromise.

December 7. Japan achieves complete surprise in its attack on Pearl Harbor. In less than two hours, the Japanese sink or damage twenty-one American vessels and destroy 165 planes. American casualties number 2,403 dead and 1,178 wounded.

November 20. Nomura presents Proposal B, an alternative to Proposal A, to Hull; President Franklin D. Roosevelt drafts his own compromise.

December 1. Japanese leaders sign war document in Tokyo.

November 26. Kido Butai departs for Pearl Harbor.

November　　　　　**December**

November 23. Admiral Nagumo gives *Kido Butai* its operations orders.

December 2. Admiral Yamamoto orders *Kido Butai* to proceed with Pearl Harbor attack.

November 27. Army chief of staff George C. Marshall issues war warning to, General Walter C. Short in Pearl Harbor.

December 8, 1200 President Roosevelt asks Congress to declare a state of war existing with Japan as of December 7.

Talking Peace and Planning War

Commodore Matthew C. Perry sailed into what is now Tokyo Harbor on July 8, 1853. Matthew was the younger brother of Oliver Hazard Perry, famous for reporting "We have met the enemy and they are ours"[1] after the Battle of Lake Erie in 1813. Matthew Perry's party consisted of four ships of war and 560 seamen.

The younger Perry came to Japan bearing a message from U.S. president Millard Fillmore. The message, a letter written by Secretary of State Daniel Webster in the form of a request, was in reality an American demand that Japan open its doors to Western trade. The letter said in part:

> Our steamships can go from California to Japan in eighteen days. . . . If your Imperial Majesty were so far to change the ancient laws as to allow free trade between the two countries, it would be extremely beneficial to both. . . . It sometimes happens in stormy weather that one of our ships is wrecked on your Imperial Majesty's shores. In all such cases we ask and expect, that our unfortunate people should be treated with kindness, and that their property should be protected, till we can send a vessel and bring them away. We are very much in earnest in this. . . . We understand there is a great abundance of coal and provisions in the empire of Japan. . . . We wish that our steamships and other vessels should be allowed to stop in Japan and supply themselves with coal, provisions and water. They will pay for them, in money, or anything else your Imperial Majesty's subjects may prefer. . . . We are very desirous of this.[2]

Without the military capability to contest President Fillmore's "gunboat diplomacy," Japan consented to the American request. Perry returned a year later to sign the Treaty of Kanagawa with Japanese shogun Iyesada.

JAPAN BECOMES A MAJOR MILITARY POWER

The Japanese opened their ports to Western trade and began to build a formidable army and navy. The ancient, isolated kingdom of Japan then became exposed to Western culture, industry, and military systems. Japan adopted a new self-image and started to dream of empire and expansion. In the brief span of eighty-eight years, Japan built, trained, and equipped an army and navy equal to those of the major European nations.

Along the way to becoming a world-class power, Japan broke out of its isolation and began to test its growing military strength. Spurred by emerging militant leaders, Japan attacked China following a disagreement over Korea. Japan quickly defeated China in the ensuing Sino-Japanese War (1894–1895) and took possession of Formosa (Taiwan) and the Pescadores. The victory established the small island nation as a major military power.

THE BATTLE OF TSUSHIMA

Nine years later, the Russo-Japanese War (1904–1905) erupted because of disputed claims over Korea and Manchuria. When Japanese forces began to prevail in the war, Russian czar Nicholas II sent his Baltic Fleet to the Orient. The czar hoped that the additional sea power might reverse the flow of battle. It did not.

Admiral Zinovy P. Rozhdestvenski, aboard the battleship *Suvorov*, commanded the Baltic group. His fleet consisted of eight battleships, eight cruisers, nine destroyers, and about twenty smaller craft. All of the vessels were either old or aging, capable as a fleet of making only nine knots under full steam. The Russian ships reached the entrance of Tsushima Strait on May 26, 1905,

Commodore Matthew C. Perry (left). Below, Perry and his delegation meet with Japanese royal commissioners to discuss the U.S. request for Japan to open trade with Western countries.

more than seven months after departing their Baltic ports. Rozhdestvenski entered the strait the next day.

Within the strait that separates the Tsushima Islands from Kyūshū and Honshū (the southeast part of the Korea Strait), the Japanese fleet awaited Rozhdestvenski's arrival. Commanded by Admiral Heihachirō Tōgō, aboard the battleship *Mikasa*, the Japanese fleet consisted of four battleships, eight cruisers, twenty-one destroyers, and sixty torpedo boats.

Admiral Tōgō enjoyed several advantages. He was fighting in home waters. His ships were newer and faster than those of his enemy, capable of fifteen-knot speeds. And his personnel were superior to the Russians in gunnery, discipline, and leadership.

The battle commenced in early afternoon, at a range of about sixty-four hundred yards. Tōgō maneuvered his faster fleet masterfully. By sundown, Rozhdestvenski had been wounded and three Russian battleships, including *Suvorov*, were sunk. Three more Russian ships were sunk during the night. Action continued into the following day. The remaining Russian ships fled toward their Pacific naval base at Vladivostok in southeast Asian Russia, pursued closely by Tōgō's fleet.

Three Russian destroyers reached Vladivostok safely. One Russian cruiser and two destroyers made safe harbor at Manila, where they were interned, or confined, for the duration of the war. All other Russian ships were sunk or captured. The Japanese lost only three torpedo boats. Russian casualties totaled ten

As depicted in this painting, the Japanese fleet soundly defeats the Russians at the Battle of Tsushima during the Russo-Japanese War.

thousand killed or wounded. Japanese losses numbered fewer than one thousand men.

The Battle of Tsushima Strait was hailed as the greatest naval battle since Britain's Lord Admiral Horatio Nelson defeated a combined French and Spanish fleet one hundred years earlier at Cape Trafalgar. Admiral Tōgō emerged from the engagement as a great and much-honored national hero. As a result of his quick victory, Japan acquired possession of the southern half of Sakhalin Island and Port Arthur. A young Japanese ensign destined for future acclaim lost two fingers of his left hand during the fray. His name was Isoroku Yamamoto.

ADVANCING JAPAN'S FORTUNES

The Japanese continued to flex their military muscles and annexed Korea in 1910. In 1914 Japan entered World War I on the side of the Allies. Japanese forces played a minor role in the Pacific, occupying German ports and colonies in the Caroline, Marshall, and Mariana Islands.

After the war, as a member of the League of Nations, Japan was awarded mandate over the Caroline and Marshall Islands and the Marianas, except for Guam (which was ceded to the United States by Spain in 1898).

The United States, Great Britain, and Japan emerged from World War I as the world's three greatest naval powers. Each of the three nations immediately embarked on a course aimed at making its own navy the world's dominant sea power. But Japan's World War I Allies slyly took measures to limit Japanese naval presence in the Pacific.

In November 1921, Charles Evans Hughes, U.S. secretary of state, convened a disarmament meeting among the Allies—the United States, Britain, France, Italy, and Japan—known as the Washington Naval Conference. Out of this conference came the Washington Treaty, signed in February of the following year. With this treaty, Japan reluctantly agreed to a capital ship tonnage ratio of five for the United States, five for Great Britain, and three for Japan (5-5-3). The majority powers ostensibly reasoned that Japan, operating only in the Pacific Ocean, required a smaller navy than either the United States, with two oceans to patrol, or Britain, with a presence in all oceans.

This agreement allotted a total tonnage of 525,000 tons for capital ships (warships with more than 10,000 tons of water displacement and fitted with eight-inch or heavier guns) and aircraft carriers to the United States and Great Britain, while limiting Japan to 315,000 tons. (The total tonnage for aircraft carriers was 135,000 tons each for the United States and Britain and 81,000 tons for Japan.) Such an imbalance proved to be unpopular with many Japanese, who interpreted the treaty terms as a legal admission of Japan's naval inferiority to the Western powers. They felt certain that the Western nations would never concede equal status to their nation.

EVOLUTION OF JAPANESE MILITARY PLANNING

In Midway, *Mitsuo Fuchida and Masatake Okumiya explain the prewar development of Japanese strategy.*

"For many years prior to Pearl Harbor, it had been common knowledge among the rank and file of Japanese citizens that the Imperial Navy was building up its strength and formulating its strategy with the United States Navy as the hypothetical antagonist, while at the same time the Imperial Army based its preparedness and planning on the hypothesis of a contest with the Russian Army. . . .

Having fought on the side of the victorious Allies, Japan emerged from World War I a first-class world power and thus became the rival of her erstwhile companion in arms, the United States, for primacy in the Pacific. At the same time the Communist Revolution in Russia reduced the threat of Russian imperialism in Asia and relegated the new Soviet state to a place of secondary importance in Japanese military planning.

Accordingly, the new Imperial Defense Policy adopted in 1918 designated the United States as potential enemy No. 1, and the U.S.S.R. as potential enemy No. 2, for purposes of future preparedness. From that time onward, the Navy program was geared to this policy."

Two years later, the United States affronted them again by passing an immigration act barring Japanese and certain other nationalities from entering the country. The Japanese now looked on the United States as the chief obstacle to fulfilling their dreams of empire, and anti-Western feelings intensified.

The seeds of Japanese resentment sowed by the terms of the Washington Treaty in 1922, and the U.S. immigration slight two years later, soon took root in Japan's secret shipbuilding program. In a 1934 letter to a junior officer, Admiral Isoroku Yamamoto, then commander of the Japanese First Naval Air Division, summed up the views of many of his high-ranking naval colleagues. He noted that there was

an immeasurable difference [between] Japan's strength now compared with the time of the Washington Conference, and I feel keenly that the time has come for this mighty empire rising in the east to devote itself, with all due circumspection [caution], to advancing its own fortunes. The example afforded before the Great War [World War I] by Germany—which if only it had exercised forbearance for another five or ten years would by now be unrivalled in Europe—suggests that the task facing us now is to build up our strength calmly and with circumspection.[3]

In less than two decades, Japan's covert shipbuilding program would yield the world's third-largest navy. As the strength of Japan's navy grew, so too did Japanese desires for expansion into the "southern region" (or "southern resources area")—the navy's term for French Indochina, the Dutch East Indies, Malaya, and the mandated islands of the Pacific.

JAPAN EXPANDS DOMAIN

Japan started to devise a master plan that would enable it to dominate Southeast Asia and the western half of the Pacific. The plan's success required the removal of all Western influence from this area, known to the Japanese as the "greater East Asia coprosperity sphere." This sphere stretched from the Kuril Islands southeast to the Marshall Islands, west to the Dutch East Indies, and in a sweeping arc to India.

In 1931 Japan moved again to expand its domain by invading Manchuria and establishing the Japanese-controlled puppet state of Manchukuo. In July 1937, Japanese troops in Manchukuo crossed the border into China and confronted Chinese troops at the Marco Polo Bridge near Peiping (Beijing). An ensuing firefight ignited a full-scale war. Referred to as the China Incident by the Japanese, this conflict came to be known by the world as the second Sino-Japanese War.

"THE LAST REMAINING DOOR"

Japan, a small island nation, has long been concerned with too many people occupying too little space with too little food. Upon Japan's seizure of Manchuria in 1931, one Japanese army officer (quoted in Robert B. Edgerton, Warriors of the Rising Sun) *offered this explanation:*

"There are only three ways left to Japan to escape from the pressure of its surplus population. . . . The first door, emigration, has been barred to us by the anti-Japanese immigration policies of other countries. The second door, to world markets, is being pushed shut by tariff barriers and the abrogation of commercial treaties. What should Japan do when two of the three doors have been closed against her? It is quite natural that Japan should rush upon the last remaining door [territorial expansion]."

Japan quickly occupied a large section of eastern China, including China's capital at Peiping and most major Chinese seaports. When the League of Nations subsequently protested the Japanese aggression, Japan promptly resigned its membership.

Continuing its unrelenting advances toward the southern resources area—the sphere area richest in oil and other raw materials—Japan seized Hainan Island in February 1939. And with the consent of Nazi-controlled Vichy France, Japanese troops occupied northern Indochina in June 1940.

Japan next moved to show its contempt for the United States (and Great Britain, Russia, and their allies) by signing the Tripartite Pact with Germany and Italy in Berlin in September 1940. The pact called for the three nations to mutually defend one another "if attacked by a power at present not involved in the European war or in the Sino-Japanese conflict."[4] Clearly, the sole nation "not involved" with the

Japanese troops invade China during the second Sino-Japanese War. The conflict, which began in 1937, added most of eastern China to Japan's territory.

potential for attacking Japan could only mean the United States.

At the time of the signing, *Asahi Shimbun*, Tokyo's largest newspaper, predicted:

> It seems inevitable that a collision should occur between Japan, determined to establish a sphere of influence in East Asia, including the Southwest Pacific, and the United States, which is determined to meddle in the affairs on the other side of a vast ocean by every means short of war.[5]

Two Choices

When Japan occupied all of Indochina by midsummer of 1941, the United States became gravely alarmed. President Franklin D. Roosevelt acted swiftly to curb further Japanese advances in Asia, clamping a total embargo on Japan and freezing all Japanese assets in the United States. Admiral Kichisaburo Nomura, Japan's ambassador in Washington, D.C., began "to have misgivings about the future." He noted that "once the economic freeze was on, the road to a full diplomatic break [between Japan and the United States] was not long."[6] Japan immediately sent a team of diplomats to the United States to mediate the mounting disputes between the two countries.

Japan had to choose between two options. The first was to meet American demands to withdraw Japanese troops from China and halt expansion in the Far East. The second option was to continue the war in China and risk war with the United States, and most likely with Great Britain and the Netherlands as well.

While diplomats in Washington were discussing peaceful solutions to Japanese-American disagreements, militarists in Japan were completing plans for a surprise attack on Pearl Harbor.

Chapter

1 Japan Decides on War

The aircraft carriers and their escorts steamed steadily through the wintry waters of the northern Pacific. Gale-force winds and huge waves tossed them about mightily. They had crossed a large expanse of ocean on the way to their destination, forty miles northeast of Kahuku Point on the island of Oahu, Hawaii, and arrived on the seventh day of the month. A half hour before dawn, the carriers launched 152 airplanes for an attack on military bases at Pearl Harbor and surrounding areas. It was a Sunday morning.

Base commanders on Oahu had been warned to expect some kind of attack. Yet when the carrier planes roared out of the rain clouds that capped the Koolau Range, they caught the Ford Island Naval Air Station, the army's Hickam and Wheeler Fields, and the Wailupe radio station by surprise. No defensive aircraft rose to meet the brazen attackers. All the attackers returned safely to their carriers to complete a most successful mission. A later judgment credited the raiders with inflicting enormous destruction across the undefended island.

HOW TO OPEN HOSTILITIES

Was this the judgment of Japan's sneak attack on Pearl Harbor on December 7, 1941? Not at all. This was the assessment of American military analysts following the Grand Joint Army and Navy Exercise carried out in Hawaiian waters on February 7, 1932.

This exercise involved a major portion of the U.S. Pacific Fleet and, according to official records, was intended

> to train the two Services in the joint operation involved in the defense of such an area. More specifically it is to determine the effectiveness of the air, surface, sub-surface and land defenses of Hawaii to repel such an attack.[7]

Rear Admiral Harry E. Yarnell, commander of the navy's attack force, shunned traditional naval strategy that relied on battleships and cruisers as offensive mainstays. In directing the mock attack on Pearl Harbor, the air-minded and forward-looking Yarnell served notice that the aircraft carrier would soon replace the battleship as the principal ship in the navies of the world.

Leaving battleships and cruisers behind, he raced across the Pacific from California with the carriers *Lexington* and *Saratoga* and a destroyer escort. Although alert to the imminence of an attack, the military installations on Oahu had expected an attack more in keeping with conventional naval practices. Admiral Yarnell's carrier-based air strike at dawn caught Oahu's defenders totally by surprise and achieved great success.

This demonstration of the island's defensive unreadiness should have sounded a warning note to responsible American military leaders, but the note went unheard or at least unheeded. Naval strategists of that time believed that the presence of battleships would sharply limit carriers in their freedom of movement. The prevailing attitude, therefore, was to assign carriers to perform only an auxiliary role in naval warfare.

Discounting the powerful performance of Yarnell's carriers, the chief umpire of the training exercise concluded:

> It is doubtful if air attacks can be launched against Oahu in the face of strong defensive aviation without subjecting carriers to the danger of material damage and consequent great losses to the attacking air force.[8]

Rear Admiral Harris Laning, one of the umpires for the exercise, also discounted

Rear Admiral Harry E. Yarnell used the aircraft carriers Lexington *and* Saratoga *(pictured here off the shore of Honolulu) to launch the 1932 mock attack on Pearl Harbor.*

"No Over–All Defense"

Admiral Yarnell's successful mock attack on Pearl Harbor in 1932 went unheeded. Another similar U.S. training exercise held in April of the following year showed no improvement in Hawaiian defenses. Amazingly, six more years elapsed without any serious American effort to bolster Hawaii's defenses against a possible surprise air attack. This neglect alarmed U.S. Army Air Corps general H. H. "Hap" Arnold during a visit to Hawaii in 1939. In this excerpt from John Toland's Infamy, *Arnold warns Americans of this seeming invitation to disaster.*

"On our return to Washington [he wrote] I was quoted by the newspaper commentators as having said I would have liked nothing better than to have a chance to take a crack at Pearl Harbor from the air with all those ships lying at anchor. Whether I really said it or not, the target presented was an airman's dream—a concentration difficult to find. But worse, it seemed to me—though about this I could say nothing publicly—was the lack of unity of command in Hawaii. Here the dismal idea of 'responsibility of the Army and the Navy being divided at the shoreline' was as sadly evident as I had ever seen it. Actually, nobody was in over–all command, and thus there was no over–all defense."

the possibility of a real attack. "As long as our fleet exists," he said with conviction, "no enemy is likely to make such an attack as this was."[9]

The Japanese thought otherwise. In 1936 their Navy War College published a *Study of Strategy and Tactics in Operations Against the United States.* The study stated, "In case the enemy's main fleet is berthed at Pearl Harbor, the idea should be to open hostilities by surprise attacks from the air."[10] So began Japanese preparations for the infamous attack on Pearl Harbor that drew the United States into World War II.

The Fate of Japan

Following the Washington Naval Conference of 1921–1922, the Japanese navy called its own conference and defined the empire's naval mission: to secure command of the western Pacific. Japanese naval planners focused at once on what they called the "great all-out battle strategy." This strategy was intended to lure the U.S. fleet into Japan's home waters, where Japanese submarines could whittle it down to a size comparable to Japan's fleet. At some prearranged spot, the Japanese navy would then engage the American navy in an all-out battle for mastery of the Pacific.

Japan felt that this strategy would enable its navy to overcome the numerical disadvantage resulting from the ship-building restrictions imposed by the Washington Naval Conference. To implement this plan, Japan built a fleet designed to operate in waters close to home, with ships that emphasized speed and firepower rather than range and armor. Over the years, most high-level officials of the Japanese navy concurred in this strategy of luring the U.S. Navy into Japanese waters. One major figure did not agree: Admiral Isoroku Yamamoto.

Yamamoto, commander in chief of the Combined (Japanese) Fleet, began considering a strike against the U.S. Pacific Fleet at Pearl Harbor in May 1940. Having attended Harvard and served as naval attaché in Washington, D.C., in the 1920s, he had grown to like Americans and had gained great respect for America's industrial potential. Reluctant to chart a collision course with a nation potentially much stronger than Japan, Yamamoto opposed a war with the United States. He warned his compatriots:

> If it is necessary to fight, in the first six months to a year of war against the United States and England I will run wild. But I must also tell you that if the war be prolonged for two or three years I have no confidence in our ultimate victory.[11]

Moreover, Yamamoto questioned the wisdom and motives of Japan's political leaders. His reluctance should never be mistaken for fear, however, for Yamamoto was first, last, and always a patriot of unsurpassed courage.

On December 10, 1940, Yamamoto frankly voiced his growing bitterness in a letter to Vice Admiral Shigetaro Shimada, a former classmate at the naval academy:

> The present government seems to be in complete confusion. Its action in showing surprise now at America's economic pressure and fuming and complaining against it reminds me of the aimless action of a schoolboy which has no more consistent motive than the immediate need or whim of the moment. . . . It would be extremely dangerous for the [Japanese] Navy to make any move in the belief that such

Admiral Isoroku Yamamoto, commander in chief of the Combined (Japanese) Fleet.

At the Very Outset

In January 1941, Admiral Isoroku Yamamoto, commander in chief of the Japanese Combined Fleet, sent a private letter to Rear Admiral Takijiro Onishi, chief of staff of the Eleventh Air Fleet. The contents of that letter would set in motion an undertaking that would change the world before the end of the year. The letter (reprinted in Goldstein and Dillon, The Pearl Harbor Papers*) contained the following request:*

"In the event of outbreak of war with the United States, there would be little prospect of our operations succeeding unless, at the very outset, we can deal a crushing blow to the main force of the American Fleet in Hawaiian waters by using the full strength of the 1st and 2nd air Squadrons against it, and thus to preclude the possibility of the American Fleet advancing to take the offensive in the Western Pacific for some time.

And it is my hope that I may be given command of this air attack force, so that I may carry out the operation myself. Please make a study of the operation."

---

men as Prince Konoye and Foreign Minister Matsuoka can be relied upon.

Nor did Yamamoto believe for one moment that negotiations could resolve Japanese-American differences:

> Nomura [Japan's ambassador in Washington, D.C.,] has no confidence that he will succeed in his mission, and besides, it is expecting too much to adjust our relations with America through diplomacy at this late stage.

Yamamoto concluded his letter to Shimada by cautioning that

> If . . . it is felt that war cannot be avoided, it would be best to decide on war with America from the beginning and to begin by taking the Philippines,

thereby reducing the line of operations and assuring the sound execution of operations. . . . The southern operations, unlike the operations in China, will determine the nation's rise or fall, for they will lead to a war in which the nation's very fate will be at stake.[12]

Despite Yamamoto's reluctance to fight the Americans, no one could doubt that he would serve his country well if war broke out. As developing events would soon dictate, the reluctant admiral would hold the fate of Japan in his hands.

Demonstration at Taranto

In January 1941, as war with the West moved ever closer to becoming a reality,

Yamamoto secretly initiated a serious study for a surprise attack on Pearl Harbor. To assist in the study of what he termed Operation Hawaii, Yamamoto called on his chief of staff, Rear Admiral Shigeru Fukudome, to find him an air officer "whose past career has not influenced him in conventional operations."[13]

In strict secrecy, Fukudome contacted Rear Admiral Takijiro Onishi, then serving as chief of staff to the commander of the navy's land-based air force. Onishi faced many problems in his new assignment. One of his chief tasks was to devise a way to launch aerial torpedoes in the shallow waters of Pearl Harbor. Existing torpedoes would either bottom out in Pearl's forty-foot depths or smack the water and bounce harmlessly over the decks of targeted vessels. Admiral Onishi immediately enlisted the help of Commander Minoru Genda, a brilliant young air officer who had recently returned from attaché duty in London. Genda accepted the task with enthusiasm.

While in London, Genda had learned much about the Royal Air Force's (RAF) daring raid on the Italian fleet at its Taranto anchorage. On the night of November 11–12, 1940, the British aircraft carrier *Illustrious* had plowed through the Mediterranean Sea under the cover of darkness. About 170 miles southeast of Italy's heel, a dozen obsolescent Fairey Swordfish biplanes took off from the three-inch-thick steel decks of the world's first fully armored carrier.

Led by Lieutenant Commander Kenneth Williamson, the flimsy Swordfish carried mixed ordnance (weapons and equipment): Six were armed with torpedoes (modified with wooden fins for Taranto Harbor's shallow, eighty-foot depths), four with bombs, and two with a split load of bombs and flares for lighting up the target area. The twelve old and frail biplanes assembled overhead and headed northwest, toward a historic rendezvous with the unsuspecting

On the night of November 11–12, 1940, Britain sent Fairey Swordfish torpedo planes (right) from the aircraft carrier Illustrious *(left) to attack the Italian fleet at Taranto.*

THE KNOX REPORT

On Sunday morning, December 7, 1941, the New York Times *carried the following front-page headlines: "NAVY IS SUPERIOR TO ANY, SAYS KNOX . . . SECRETARY'S ANNUAL REPORT CITES COMMISSIONING OF 325 NEW SHIPS, 2059 PLANES." The related story, datelined Washington, December 6 (taken from Prange, Goldstein, and Dillon,* Pearl Harbor: The Verdict of History), *reported,*

"The United States Navy, now in the midst of a record expansion program and recently placed on a war footing with full personnel manning the ships of three fleets, has at this time no superior in the world, Secretary [Frank] Knox stated tonight in rendering the annual report of the Navy Department.

'I am proud to report,' Secretary Knox wrote, 'that the American people may feel fully confident in their Navy. In my opinion, the loyalty, morale and technical ability of the personnel are without superior. On any comparable basis, the United States Navy is second to none.'"

Italian fleet. Another wave of nine Swordfish would follow an hour later.

The lumbering biplanes split up at the approaches to the Italian naval base, hoping to confuse the antiaircraft gunners. Ignoring a constant barrage of protective antiaircraft fire over the heavily defended Italian anchorage, the Swordfish plunged to the attack. Their two-wave assault left behind three Italian battleships in sinking condition, two cruisers badly damaged, and two fleet auxiliary ships sunk— about half of Italy's fleet strength. The British lost only two of their twenty-one aircraft.

The remaining ships of the Italian fleet fled from the high seas to seek safe harbor in Naples. Commenting on the daring raid by carrier-based planes, British prime minister Winston Churchill later wrote:

> By this single stroke the balance of naval power in the Mediterranean was decisively altered. . . . Half the Italian battle fleet was disabled for at least six months, and the [British] Fleet Air Arm could rejoice at having seized by their gallant exploit one of the rare opportunities presented to them.[14]

At Taranto, Britain's naval aviators demonstrated for the first time the effectiveness of carrier-based aircraft used as a weapon against a fleet of warships. The stunning British success—and its significance—did not go unnoticed in either the United States or Japan, especially in Japan. Both Yamamoto and Genda now felt certain that Japan could execute a similar successful attack against the U.S. Pacific Fleet at Pearl Harbor. At Yamamoto's request, the talented young Genda began preparing a plan.

Knox Issues a Clear Warning

At the same time, U.S. secretary of the navy Frank Knox also recognized the significance of the Taranto raid. He sent a warning message (drafted by then captain Richmond Kelly Turner) to Secretary of War Henry L. Stimson, stating in part, "If war eventuates with Japan, it is believed easily possible that hostilities would be initiated by a surprise attack upon the Fleet or the Naval Base at Pearl Harbor."[15]

Stimson agreed and passed the message (which included Knox's suggestions for appropriate countermeasures) along to Admiral Husband E. Kimmel, commander in chief of the Pacific Fleet (CinC-PAC), at Pearl Harbor. Kimmel opposed suggestions for installing torpedo nets to protect his ships, arguing that nets would interfere with ship movements within the tight confines of the harbor. He also arrogantly rejected any suggestion that Japan might undertake a venture so far from home with its (supposedly) inferior aircraft and pilots.

Admiral James O. Richardson, commander in chief of the United States Fleet (CinCUS), shared Kimmel's view. He simply could not believe that the Japanese would attack American ships or their base. Nor did he feel the need to take extra precautions against an unlikely torpedo attack.

On January 7, 1941, in a memorandum to Chief of Naval Operations (CNO) Harold R. Stark, Richardson wrote:

> There does not appear to be any practicable way of placing torpedo baffles or nets within the harbor to protect ships moored therein against torpedo plane attack without greatly limiting the activities within the harbor. . . . Inasmuch as Pearl harbor is the only operating base available to the Fleet in this area any passive defense measures that will further restrict the use of the base as such should be avoided. Considering this and the improbability of such an attack under present conditions and the unlikelihood of an enemy being able to advance carriers sufficiently near in wartime in the face of active Fleet operations, it is not considered necessary to lay such nets.[16]

The Japanese, on the other hand, could not conceive of the Americans failing to take such precautions. They tried mightily to learn where the U.S. Navy might have installed torpedo nets in Pearl Harbor. Their efforts failed because the U.S. Navy had not installed any such nets—nets that might have spared the United States great damage to capital ships and untold casualties.

The navy's high command, through overconfidence in its own defensive capabilities and disbelief in a potential Japanese threat, failed to heed Frank Knox's clear warning.

OPPOSITION TO YAMAMOTO'S PLAN

In March 1941 Commander Genda completed a plan for Admiral Yamamoto's Operation Hawaii. Admiral Onishi reviewed Genda's plan and gave it a 60 percent chance of success. But Onishi's superior, Admiral Fukudome, allowed the plan only a 40 percent success rating.

It now became Yamamoto's turn to review Genda's proposal. He liked it.

Though still opposed to a war with the United States, Yamamoto saw Operation Hawaii—a first crippling strike against the enemy—as the only assurance of Japan's success in the short run. He now took an active role in many tasks. His multiple duties included overseeing the preparation of a detailed plan, putting together the right mix of people, organizing and training fleet units, developing special ordnance, and convincing other high-level Japanese naval officers that his plan would work. The latter task threatened to be the hardest of the lot.

The general staff of the Imperial Japanese navy (which held the ultimate responsibil-

U.S. secretary of the navy Frank Knox issued a warning about the threat of an attack on Pearl Harbor.

U.S. president Franklin D. Roosevelt vowed to defeat Nazi Germany, a declaration Japan took as a threat to Japanese expansion.

ity for naval operations) did not agree with Yamamoto's plan; they said it was too risky. Their opinion gained strength when a war-games exercise held in Tokyo in September 1941 tried out the plan. Results of the exercise showed a paper loss of two Japanese aircraft carriers.

Meanwhile, in a Labor Day radio broadcast on September 1, 1941, President Franklin D. Roosevelt assured the American public that the United States possessed "a strong Navy, a Navy gaining in strength." He further declared that Americans would "do everything in [their] power

to crush Hitler and his Nazi forces."[17] President Roosevelt did not mention Japan in his speech. But the Japanese interpreted his threat against the Nazis as a threat against further Japanese expansion as well.

Two days later, Prince Fumimaro Konoye, Japan's premier, called a liaison meeting between members of the Japanese cabinet and the foreign ministry to discuss the "Outline Plan for the Execution of the Empire's National Policy." After much haggling over wording, their discussion yielded a historic statement of Japanese policy. The statement declared, in part:

Emperor Hirohito approved Japan's policy to go to war against the United States, Britain, and the Netherlands if necessary.

I. Our Empire, for the purpose of self-defense and self-preservation, will complete preparations for war, with the last ten days of October as a tentative deadline, resolved to go to war with the United States, Great Britain and the Netherlands if necessary.

II. Our Empire will concurrently take all possible diplomatic measures [in relation to] the United States and Great Britain, and thereby endeavor to obtain our objectives. . . .

III. In the event that there is no prospect of our demands being met by the first ten days of October through the diplomatic negotiations mentioned above, we will immediately decide to commence hostilities against the United States, Britain and the Netherlands.[18]

The Japanese cabinet approved this policy on September 4, 1941, as did Emperor Hirohito two days later. Nonetheless, arguments persisted between Yamamoto and the general staff as to how to proceed.

FUKUDOME'S ALARM

Vice Admiral Shigeru Fukudome, Yamamoto's chief of staff during the plan's conceptual stage, later became one of the plan's severest critics. Fukudome, upon promotion to chief of staff of the general staff's First Bureau in October 1941, said that the plan was too risky. In a meeting with Admiral Osami Nagano, chief of the naval general staff, and Nagano's vice chief, Vice Admiral Seiichi Ito, Fukudome reported his reasons for alarm.

Rear Admiral Sadatoshi Tomioka, chief of the operations section of the naval general staff, and other officers of his section also viewed the plan with skepticism. In his postwar memoirs, Fukudome cited the following risks as being alarming and unacceptable in the consensus:

1. Surprise, the key to the plan's success, would be difficult to achieve. It was all too likely that secrecy might be compromised by foreign intelligence agents, chance meetings with other ships on the high seas, and American reconnaissance.

2. Japan's traditional strategy, predicated on a gradual American advance through the Japanese-controlled Mandates (the Marshall, Mariana, and Caroline Islands) followed by a decisive battle near the homeland, was still sound. There was no compelling need to eliminate the U.S. fleet before seizing Southeast Asia.

3. Operational difficulties were formidable. Maintaining radio silence and refueling at sea offered too many chances for the plan to go awry.

4. Diplomatic negotiations aimed at averting war were still in progress. Japanese naval officers were under no illusions about their chances for success in a war against the United States. A surprise attack on Pearl Harbor would dash any remaining hope of peace.[19]

Admirals Nagano and Ito particularly shared Fukudome's alarm. Some staff members favored striking south and attacking America only in self-defense—that is, only in the event that the U.S. fleet ventured westward out of Pearl Harbor. Given Japan's intent to take over the Philippines, that show of U.S. sea power would surely occur.

In answer to Yamamoto's arguments, the general staff sent him a detailed paper listing several major objections to Operation Hawaii. The staff's chief concern was the real possibility of incurring enormous Japanese casualties should the attack not be a surprise. Yamamoto, in a last-ditch effort to salvage his plan, responded in dramatic fashion to his critics.

YAMAMOTO'S RESPONSE

On October 18, 1941, the general staff met again in Tokyo to consider war plans. Yamamoto sent Captain Kameto Kuroshima, his senior staff officer, to represent him. As Yamamoto's agent, Kuroshima faced a difficult, dual task: First, he had to obtain the staff's approval for Operation Hawaii, and second, he had to secure a firm commitment that the First Air Fleet's six carriers would be available for the Pearl Harbor attack.

Kuroshima arrived in Tokyo carrying a secret weapon to help turn aside his opposition. When Rear Admiral Sadatoshi Tomioka renewed his opposition to Operation Hawaii, Kuroshima unleashed the secret weapon. He told the general staff that, failing the acceptance of Yamamoto's plan, the admiral "must resign his position and retire into civilian life."[20] In that event, Yamamoto's staff would also resign.

Kuroshima's declaration so stunned Tomioka that he took the matter to his superior, Vice Admiral Fukudome, formerly

An aerial view of Pearl Harbor just weeks before the attack. On November 5, 1941, Admiral Yamamoto issued Operation Order No. 1, which commenced Operation Hawaii.

Yamamoto's chief of staff and now chief of the naval general staff's First (Operations) Bureau. Fukudome in turn elevated the matter to Vice Admiral Seiichi Ito, vice chief of the naval general staff. Ito brought the issue straight to Admiral Osami Nagano, chief of the naval general staff. Kuroshima repeated Yamamoto's ultimatum to each commander along the way and finally to Nagano. Rather than lose the services of their revered and respected commander and his loyal staff, the general staff finally yielded to Yamamoto's demands, and all arguments ended.

OPERATION HAWAII COMMENCES

On November 5, 1941, Yamamoto issued Operation Order No. 1, which stated, in part:

In the East the American fleet will be destroyed. The American lines of operation and supply lines to the Orient will be cut. Enemy forces will be intercepted and annihilated. Victories will be exploited to break the enemy's will to fight.[21]

Yamamoto then set Sunday, December 7, 1941, as the date of the Pearl Harbor attack. The date was then designated X day, the Japanese equivalent of D day (a day set for launching an operation). He selected a Sunday because he knew that Americans like to relax on weekends and that most of the U.S. fleet put into the harbor on weekends.

Operation Hawaii was on.

2 Under Way to Infamy

Although Yamamoto's proposal to attack Pearl Harbor was not approved until November 1941, advanced planning and intense preparations for Operation Hawaii —now renamed Operation Z—had begun in April of that year. The attack plan drafted by Commander Minoru Genda in February served as a beacon to guide Yamamoto and his Combined Fleet through the perilous waters that lay ahead.

MINORU GENDA

Military historians often refer to Commander Minoru Genda as a Japanese Billy Mitchell. William "Billy" Mitchell, a visionary American army officer during the early days of aviation, is generally considered to be the father of the U.S. Air Force. It is with good reason that Genda, who was also an aviator and aerial tactician of great vision, should be compared to Mitchell. Both men recognized the potential of airpower and foresaw the demise of the battleship.

In mid-1936, while a student officer at the Navy War College in Tokyo, Genda proclaimed:

The main strength of a decisive battle should be air arms, while its auxiliary should be built mostly by submarines. Cruisers and destroyers will be employed as screens of carrier groups,

Commander Minoru Genda (seen here in 1940) believed airpower would render battleships obsolete.

while battleships will be put out of commission and tied up.

Continuing, Genda wrote:

> The basic concept to support this assertion was obviously a flat denial of the hitherto long cherished concept of a sea battle . . . a concept which was built on an idea of waging once and for all a decisive gunfire engagement with battleships as the nucleus of strength. Instead, it [Genda's concept] aimed at launching a fatal series of aerial attacks upon enemy fleets from carrier groups operating a few hundred miles away from the enemy force, while land-based air forces and submarines were to support them.[22]

Five years later, when Admiral Yamamoto asked the forward-thinking Genda to devise a plan for attacking Pearl Harbor, Genda's drafted response incorporated all of the features of his earlier vision.

EIGHT CRITICAL ELEMENTS

Genda's draft basically contained eight critical elements:

1. *Surprise and absolute secrecy.* The success of the operation depended on catching U.S. forces by complete surprise. Any breach of secrecy might enable the Americans to spring a trap and inflict huge damages on the Combined Fleet. Surprise was key.

2. *American carriers as primary targets.* Genda disagreed with Yamamoto's original intent of targeting American battle-ships first. The air-minded commander recognized the far-ranging destructive potential of carrier-based aircraft. By eliminating American carriers without serious damage to its own carriers, the Combined Fleet would gain a huge advantage. It could then chip away at destroying the remaining U.S. fleet, free of danger from air attacks originating from American carriers. Eventually, the Imperial Navy would dominate the vast Pacific.

3. *Destruction of U.S. aircraft on Oahu.* Genda considered control of the skies over Oahu essential to a successful mission. He hoped to catch and destroy most of the enemy's aircraft on the ground at the beginning of the attack. Control of the air would enable his own aircraft to go about their deadly tasks unopposed. It also eliminated the possibility of an American counterstrike against the Japanese carriers.

4. *The use of all available Japanese carriers.* Shunning Yamamoto's earlier tentative suggestion for using one or possibly two carrier divisions (two to four carriers), Genda insisted on using all available carriers for the attack. The military principle of mass, which entails a maximum concentration of force on an objective to yield maximum effect, guided Genda's thinking. He wanted to inflict maximum damage on the U.S. fleet. The amount of potential damage became a function of the number of available carriers. Genda eventually settled for six.

5. *The use of all types of bombing techniques—torpedo, dive, and high level—in the attack.* Although Genda favored the aerial

SHOWDOWN IN DECEMBER

Commander Minoru Genda, one of the chief architects of the Japanese plan to attack Pearl Harbor, was among the first advocates of carrier attack forces. But in the following passage (extracted from Goldstein and Dillon's The Pearl Harbor Papers*), Genda credits Admiral Isoroku Yamamoto as the driving force behind the Japanese carrier attack force.*

"In 1936, when I strongly advocated the wisdom of a task force centering around carriers, there were few supporters even among my colleague fliers, and there was always a feud between me and listeners as I argued the need of it. Even in the middle of 1941, when the same task force which eventually attacked Pearl Harbor was organized, it was a fact that most of the leading admirals and strategists in the Japanese Navy were opposed to the idea. Only because of a strong, unyielding demand by Admiral Isoroku Yamamoto, then C-in-C [commander in chief] of the Combined Fleet, who firmly believed that his strategy of launching a surprise aerial attack on Pearl Harbor at the very outset of war could only be made with concentrated air power, was the idea finally materialized.

I was at least one of the early advocates of this task force idea, and ever since had been in the center of the whirlwind which had swirled in the Japanese Navy for several years, until a showdown of the debate was decisively made in early December 1941."

torpedo as the most effective weapon against fleet targets, he questioned whether they could be launched successfully in Pearl Harbor's shallow waters. The possibility that U.S. ships might be protected by torpedo nets also concerned him. He opted for dive-bombing as a first alternative to a failed torpedo-bombing attack. Genda backed up his first two bombing choices by including high-level bombing (a high-altitude, level-flight approach) provisions in his draft.

6. *A strong fighter escort.* Genda foresaw a three fold role for a strong fighter escort. Fighters would be needed to protect Japanese bombers flying to and from their targets at Pearl Harbor. These same fighters would also be required to clear the skies of enemy aircraft. A separate fighter group would be needed to form a protective umbrella over the Japanese carrier force to prevent an enemy counterattack from the air.

7. *Refueling at sea.* The limited radius of action of most Japanese ships made refueling at sea necessary. Fuel tankers would be required to accompany the attack force. Moreover, because Japanese Navy

personnel lacked experience in refueling at sea, they would need intensive training and practice.

8. *A daylight attack.* Japanese military aircraft of that time were not equipped with adequate instruments for conducting night operations. Accordingly, Genda specified predawn launch times so that Japanese planes would arrive over Oahu at daybreak.

AN INTERESTING POSSIBILITY

While Genda and other aviators worked at developing the framework for an attack plan, Yamamoto's Combined Fleet staff was focusing on special tasks. The staff devoted particular attention to logistics, submarine warfare, navigation, and communications. Yamamoto even considered the possibility of including an invasion of Hawaii as part of his attack plan. One of Yamamoto's colleagues pointed out that half the U.S. Navy was stationed in Hawaii. The capture or elimination of that many personnel would strike a crippling—even mortal—blow to American offensive capabilities in the Pacific. It was indeed an interesting possibility, and one that Yamamoto did not entirely rule out until November.

SOMETHING NEW UNDER THE RISING SUN

The planning gained momentum and moved beyond the conceptual stage, starting with major personnel and organizational changes. On April 10, the Imperial Japanese Navy (IJN) established the First Air Fleet and in so doing took a huge stride into the future. Traditionally, aircraft carrier divisions had been deployed as part of separate battle groups under separate commands. This new organization grouped carrier divisions under a single command for the first time, marking a truly revolutionary development.

The First Air Fleet originally comprised two carrier divisions with two carriers each and a third division with one carrier. The First Carrier Division consisted of the carriers *Akagi*, flagship for both the division and the air fleet, and *Kaga*. Each carrier displaced about forty-two thousand tons. *Akagi* could make thirty-one knots; *Kaga* twenty-eight. The newer carriers *Soryu* and *Hiryu* formed the Second Carrier Division. They both displaced only thirty thousand tons but could attain thirty-four knots. The single, smaller, and slower carrier *Ryuju* made up the Fourth Carrier Division. In addition, all three divisions included two destroyers per carrier. (The Fourth Carrier Division was used for training purposes only and did not take part in the Pearl Harbor attack.) Japan's newest carriers, *Shokaku* and *Zuikaku*, joined the First Air Fleet in September to form the Fifth Carrier Division and bring the fleet's total carrier count to six. The First Air Fleet was truly something new under the rising sun.

The Japanese aircraft carriers Akagi *(left), flagship of the First Air Fleet, and* Kaga *(right).*

CHUICHI NAGUMO

To command the First Air Fleet, the navy ministry appointed Vice Admiral Chuichi Nagumo. As the housekeeping branch of the Imperial Navy, the navy ministry maintained service records and implemented promotions based on a traditional seniority system. Nagumo, with a background in battleships and cruisers, hardly seemed qualified for an aviation command. The seeming mismatch between Nagumo's experience and the requirements of his new charge was somewhat allayed later by his chief of staff, Vice Admiral Ryunosuke Kusaka:

Various criticisms have been heard about Admiral Nagumo, but I think he was after all one of our good superior officers. Though he was dauntless like a spirited horse . . . he had another side of being cautious and also rich in humanity. . . .

His ability to command units, the smartness to grasp and hold a bold decision once he made up his mind were what we subordinates had to learn from him. That he had little experience in aviation might hamper him a great deal from fully displaying his ability. It does not hit the nail on the head if we said some criticizing words taking up one or two errors or based upon hearsay.[23]

It should be noted that no one in the Japanese Navy rose to such high station without displaying great competence for many years in a variety of assignments. Nagumo, by any standard, had earned promotion to the lofty command.

In naming Kusaka to serve as Nagumo's chief of staff, the navy compensated for Nagumo's deficiencies as an air commander. Kusaka, although not an aviator, had previously captained the *Hosho* and *Akagi* on his climb up the ladder of naval air command.

Perhaps of greater consequence was the appointment of Commander Minoru Genda as Nagumo's air operations officer. Nagumo would come to rely heavily on the judgment and advice of the brilliant air tactician.

Vice Admiral Chuichi Nagumo, commander of the First Air Fleet.

Matome Ugaki, Yamamoto's chief of staff and one of Nagumo's strongest critics, wrote:

> What the hell is the attitude of the First Air Fleet? In view of the fact that it has evaded Yamamoto's plan from the beginning, it should have suggested others for the job since it could not control its subordinates.
>
> That man Nagumo—not only does he have words with others but he is given to bluffing when drunk. Even now [about five weeks before *Kido Butai*'s departure for Pearl Harbor] Nagumo is not fully prepared to send himself and his men into the jaws of death and achieve results two or three times greater than the sacrifices entailed. . . . If Nagumo and his Chief of Staff [Rear Admiral Ryunosuke Kusaka] strongly oppose this operation, and feel they cannot carry it out, they should resign their posts.[24]

With the able assistance of Kusaka and Genda, Nagumo would lead his fleet through a succession of victories. It remains doubtful, however, that Nagumo ever felt really comfortable commanding an air group. He in fact strongly opposed Operation Z in the early stages of the plan. Along with the naval general staff, Nagumo believed that fleet priorities should be directed toward securing the vital oil regions in the south.

Many officers doubted the resolve of Nagumo and his fleet to successfully execute the risky operation. Rear Admiral

Yamamoto tended to agree with Ugaki but could find no real reason to dismiss the First Air Fleet commander. In time, Nagumo eventually accepted Yamamoto's Pearl Harbor plan.

In defense of the maligned Nagumo, he pitched into his new tasks with a will and went on to compile a record of achievement unmatched by any other Japanese admiral in World War II. Whatever shortcomings and misgivings Nagumo might have displayed along the way should be measured against this record.

MITSUMI SHIMIZU

Whether from lack of total confidence in Nagumo or for some other reason, Admiral Yamamoto decided to deploy a submarine force to back up the efforts of Nagumo's aviators.

On July 29, Yamamoto consulted with Vice Admiral Mitsumi Shimizu, commander of the Sixth (submarine) Fleet. Shimizu was a good-looking man of gentle nature and calm confidence, well respected by his fellow officers and the enlisted ranks. Yamamoto approached him gravely about

Japanese submarines are seen here at anchor at the naval base in Kure, Japan. Yamamoto ordered an undersea assault force to support Nagumo's attack.

organizing and commanding an undersea assault force for Operation Z.

"Under present conditions I think war is unavoidable," Yamamoto began. "If it comes, I believe there would be nothing for me to do but attack Pearl Harbor at the outset, thus tipping the balance of power in our favor." Shimizu's mouth opened as if to speak, but he said nothing. Yamamoto hastened to acknowledge:

> I know the operation is a gamble, but I am absolutely convinced that it is the only method that can be used to meet the present situation. It will be the most effective way to hold the U.S. Fleet in check because this is what they will least expect.

Yamamoto paused briefly to allow the other man to recover from his surprise, then surprised him further. "I would like you to command our submarine forces as commander of the *Senken Butai* [Advance Force]."[25]

Although he was then commander of the Sixth Fleet, Shimizu had little personal experience as a submariner. Much of his continuing surprise derived from knowing that his great commander had chosen him over many competent high-ranking veterans of submarine warfare. Shimizu's response came from the heart: "I will do my very best to fulfill your expectations."[26]

THE COMMAND TRIANGLE

The top-level leadership structure for the Pearl Harbor plan was now established,

and it formed an odd-shaped triangle: Yamamoto, commander in chief of the Combined Fleet, stood alone at the top, a brilliant, fearless commander who approached war with the United States with severe misgivings; Nagumo, the carrier striking force leader, a shipborne torpedo expert with no expertise in air-arm (aviation) command, anchored one point on the base; and Shimizu, the submarine fleet commander with no intimate experience with submarines, held down the other base point.

With the leadership established, preparations for Operation Z moved into high gear.

UNAVAILING COURAGE

Admiral Shimizu formed a group of twenty-five submarines and five midget submarines to work independently of Nagumo's air fleet. Their duties in the impending operation would be reconnaissance, interception and destruction of American supply ships and warships attempting to move out of Pearl Harbor, and rescue of downed Japanese pilots. The midget subs were to slip into Pearl Harbor and torpedo any major warships the attacking Japanese aircraft missed.

Of all the Pearl Harbor attack forces, none drew more difficult or dangerous assignments than the courageous crews of the midget submarines. Rear Admiral Ryunosuke Kusaka later recalled some of their difficulties:

> Among those [Sixth Fleet] submarines, five took a midget submarine each on board. It was not an easy

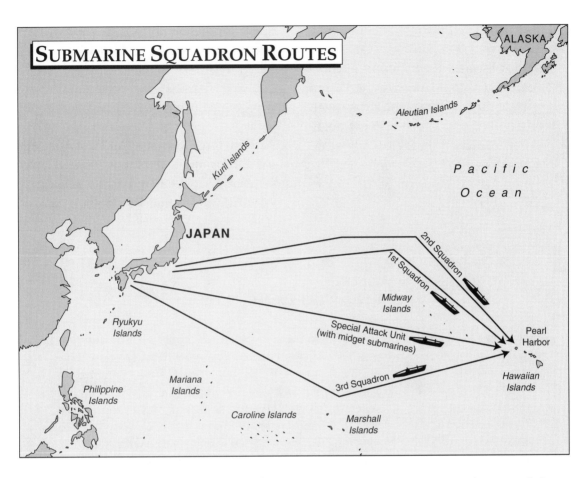

SUBMARINE SQUADRON ROUTES

ALASKA

Aleutian Islands

Kuril Islands

Pacific Ocean

JAPAN

2nd Squadron

1st Squadron

Midway Islands

Ryukyu Islands

Special Attack Unit (with midget submarines)

Pearl Harbor

3rd Squadron

Hawaiian Islands

Mariana Islands

Philippine Islands

Caroline Islands

Marshall Islands

task to make a long voyage of 3,000 miles submerging at daytime and only surfacing at night, but a more difficult task was that assigned to those young boys of the midget submarines, to whom our deepest admiration should be paid. Surely even the slightest chance of survival could hardly be seen in their assigned mission. There might be torpedo-defense nets extended along vessels, patrol boats with eagle eyes at the entrance of the bay and mine barriers laid, all of which had to be overcome to penetrate into the bay to destroy enemy vessels at one blow. When I thought

of the unsophisticated spirit of those young boys, originally I thought that the spearhead of the attack would be better made by those midget submarines. But it was decided that the initial attack be made by the air forces, lest an untimely attack by midget submarines would spoil this grave operation.

Topographically, the entrance of Pearl Harbor was so narrow that it was hard for a submarine with low view to observe clearly the enemy situation in the harbor. So it was arranged that the enemy situation in the harbor just prior to the attack be determined by *Tone*'s and *Chikuma*'s seaplanes, and the Lahaina anchorage, which could be searched from outside the anchorage, be scrutinized by a submarine in order to get negative information on the enemy situation. Most of those submarines left the homeland bases on or around 18 November.[27]

The courage of Shimizu's submariners was to far exceed their effectiveness.

YAMAMOTO'S CONVICTION

Admiral Nagumo's First Air Fleet and all its supporting units assembled in early November at Saeki Bay in Japan's Inland Sea. With Admiral Yamamoto looking on from

---

"A DIFFICULT PROPOSITION"

On November 25, 1941, in a meeting with his war cabinet, President Franklin D. Roosevelt warned that the Japanese were likely to attack the United States as early as the following Monday, December 1. Secretary of War Henry L. Stimson described the question posed by Roosevelt's warning (quoted in John Toland's The Rising Sun*).*

"The question was . . . what we should do. The question was how we could maneuver them into the position of firing the first shot without allowing too much damage to ourselves. It was a difficult proposition. U.S. secretary of state Cordell Hull laid out his general broad propositions on which the thing should be rested—the freedom of the seas and the fact that Japan was in alliance with Hitler and was carrying out his policy of world aggression. The others brought out the fact that any such expedition to the south as the Japanese were likely to take would be an encirclement of our interests in the Philippines and cutting into our vital supply of rubber from Malaysia. I pointed out to the President that he had already taken the first steps towards an ultimatum in notifying Japan way back last summer that if she crossed the border into Thailand she was violating our safety and that therefore he had only to point out [to Japan] that to follow any such expedition was a violation of a warning we had already given."

Stimson's comments should not be construed as evidence that the president had prior knowledge of the Japanese attack on Pearl Harbor but, rather, that he expected a possible attack on American territories or interests somewhere.

---

aboard his flagship *Nagato*, the fleet conducted a full dress rehearsal. An evaluation of the first rehearsal exercise indicated a need for improvement in several areas. Fleet rendezvous times, aircraft deployment and approaches to target, and torpedo launches all needed fine tuning. Two more rehearsals revealed continuing problems with torpedo launches, but further testing elevated the torpedo hits to an 82 percent success rate by mid-November.

On November 17, the one hundred officer pilots of the First Air Fleet (most prewar Japanese pilots were enlisted men) gathered aboard the *Akagi* for a final briefing from Admiral Yamamoto. He outlined the attack plan and appealed for their maximum effort. Although hoping to achieve surprise, he warned his warriors to stand ready for enormous American resistance. Because of American resourcefulness, he told them, they might be detected and have to fight their way to the target.

Yamamoto reminded them of their Bushido heritage (a warrior's code that values honor over life) and its custom of selecting an equal or stronger opponent, ending with a final word of caution. "The Americans are adversaries worthy of you,"[28] he said.

When Yamamoto finished his briefing, all those present retired to a farewell party held in *Akagi*'s wardroom. They ate the ritual fare of surume (dried cuttlefish) for happiness and kachiguri (walnuts) for victory, then toasted their emperor with sake (rice wine) and shouted, *"Banzai! Banzai! Banzai!"* ("May you live forever!").

Before leaving, Yamamoto expressed confidence in the outcome of the impending attack. He told the gathering that he expected the operation to be a success. His choice of words—*expected* rather than *hoped for* a success—subtly conveyed his conviction and gave heart to all those about to sail into harm's way.

Nagumo's Operations Orders

On November 23, Admiral Nagumo issued a set of operations orders outlining the attack plan for members of his First Air Fleet. Briefly, the final formation of Nagumo's *Kido Butai* (Striking Force) and the operational roles assigned to individual elements of the force were as follows:

• The 6 carriers, *Akagi* (Red Castle, First Air Fleet flagship), *Kaga* (Increased Joy), *Hiryu* (Flying Dragon), *Soryu* (Green Dragon), *Shokaku* (Soaring Crane), and *Zuikaku* (Happy Crane), along with their 423 aircraft (353 of which were to be used in the Pearl Harbor attack), formed the nucleus and main offensive force of Kido Butai.

• Nine destroyers and the light cruiser *Abukuma* (escort flagship) were assigned to provide protective screening for the carriers.

• The battleships *Hiei* and *Kirishima*, with the heavy cruisers *Tone* and *Chikuma*, respectively, added 14- and 8-inch guns as backup against unforeseen dangers. The cruisers also carried observation planes for scouting the Pearl Harbor area well in advance of the striking force.

• Three submarines (not part of Shimizu's group) were designated to join *Kido Butai* at sea and patrol the waters on either side and forward of the main body on the way to Pearl Harbor.

• Seven oil tankers, slated to bring up the rear for refueling en route, rounded out Nagumo's fleet.

The fleet was to gather at Etorofu Island in the Kurils, northeast of Japan's northern island of Hokkaidō, and depart eastward, refueling as necessary. Observation aircraft were to precede the attack planes and scout out both Pearl Harbor and the alternate fleet anchorage at Lahaina Roads. The carriers would then launch their attack planes from a point about two hundred miles north of Oahu in two waves thirty minutes apart. The attack would proceed in this fashion if all went as planned.

The first wave included all forty torpedo bombers, when the opportunity for surprise would be greatest. The torpedo bombers flew low and slow, and the advantage of surprise would increase their chances of survival. Each attack element was assigned a specific target. The torpedo bombers were directed to attack carrier moorings on the northwest side of Ford Island and Battleship Row on the island's southeast side. Dive-bombers of the first wave drew targets at Wheeler Field, the army air corps fighter base, and the naval air station on Ford Island.

Dive-bombers in the second wave were assigned to targets at Kaneohe Naval Air Station, the marine airfield at Ewa, and the army bomber base at Hickam Field. Fighter planes were to escort both waves and maintain control of the air. Other second-wave dive-bombers would close out the

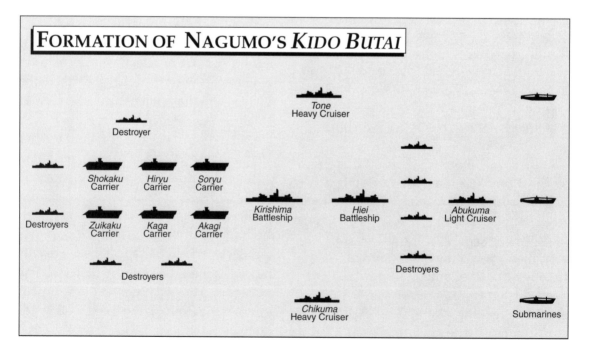

FORMATION OF NAGUMO'S *KIDO BUTAI*

Tone
Heavy Cruiser

Destroyer

Shokaku
Carrier

Hiryu
Carrier

Soryu
Carrier

Destroyers

Zuikaku
Carrier

Kaga
Carrier

Akagi
Carrier

Kirishima
Battleship

Hiei
Battleship

Abukuma
Light Cruiser

Destroyers

Destroyers

Chikuma
Heavy Cruiser

Submarines

"Glory or Oblivion"

On December 1, 1941, five days after Admiral Nagumo's Kido Butai *had sailed for Pearl Harbor, Emperor Hirohito granted final approval for Japan's war plans. In the following passage from David Bergamini's* Japan's Imperial Conspiracy, *Japanese prime minister General Hideki Tōjō responds to his emperor's decision.*

"At this moment our Empire stands at the threshold of glory or oblivion. We tremble with fear in the Presence of His Majesty. We subjects are keenly aware of the great responsibilities we must assume from this point on. Now that His Majesty has reached a decision to commence hostilities, we must all strive to repay our obligations to him, bring the Government and the military ever closer together, resolve that the nation united will go on to victory, make an all-out effort to achieve our war aims, and set His Majesty's mind at ease. I now adjourn the meeting."

General Hideki Tōjō, prime minister of Japan.

---

mission by attacking any carriers left afloat and any chance targets.

Peace Talks Continue

Shimizu's Sixth Fleet submarines started departing Japanese bases in mid-November. Nagumo's carriers and escorting vessels gathered at Etorofu as planned and commenced their eastward voyage to infamy on November 26. Yamamoto's final instructions to Nagumo were as follows: "In case negotiations with the United States reach a successful conclusion, the task force will immediately put about and return to the homeland."[29]

Meanwhile, Japanese and American diplomats continued to hold peace discussions in Washington, D.C.

3 Point of Attack

It now seems reasonable to conclude that the most surprising aspect of Japan's surprise attack on Pearl Harbor is that it came as a surprise. Evidence of Japanese intent abounded. But multiple warnings of Japan's impending actions went unnoticed or unheeded. Why? The answer now lies only slightly obscured by the trappings of miscommunications, old intrigues, and misconceptions.

A WARNING FROM TOKYO

By early November 1941, officials at the American Embassy in Tokyo were alarmed at what they judged to be an atmosphere of growing Japanese hostility toward the United States. General Hideki Tōjō, a well-known militarist and leader of Japan's Kodo-Ha war party, had been named prime minister and ordered to form a new cabinet on October 18, 1941. After evaluating Japan's new government for two weeks, Joseph C. Grew, the American ambassador in Japan, concluded that Tōjō's regime might seek a military solution.

On November 3, more than three weeks before *Kido Butai* put to sea out of Etorofu, Grew sent a cautionary note to the U.S. Department of State. He warned that if negotiations with the Japanese failed, Japan might mount an "all-out do-or-die attempt actually risking national Hara-Kiri [suicide] to make Japan impervious to economic embargoes rather than yield to foreign pressure."[30]

Ambassador Joseph C. Grew warned the United States of a possible Japanese attack.

BASIS FOR NEGOTIATIONS

On April 16, 1941, Secretary of State Cordell Hull presented a four-point basis for negotiations to Admiral Kichisaburo Nomura, the Japanese ambassador in Washington. Throughout long months of negotiations between the United States and Japan, the United States held fast to the spirit of Hull's Four Principles (as shown in John Toland's The Rising Sun).

"1. Respect for the territorial integrity and sovereignty of each and all nations.

2. Support of the principle of noninterference in the internal affairs of other countries.

3. Support of the principle of equality, including equality of commercial opportunity.

4. Nondisturbance of the status quo in the Pacific except as the status quo may be altered by peaceful means."

Ambassador Grew commented that he doubted his note would receive a "hot reception" despite its gravity. His diary entry that evening noted:

> There is a lot of talk around town to the effect that the Japanese, in case of a break with the United States, are planning to go all out in a surprise mass attack on Pearl Harbor. I rather guess that the boys in Hawaii are not precisely asleep.[31]

But as the ambassador feared, Washington failed to take his warning seriously.

A DIFFICULT ORDER

The Japanese, of course, had already decided earlier (at the Imperial Conference in Tokyo on September 6) to go to war with the United States "when necessary."[32] The Combined Fleet had accepted that decision as permission to implement its plan to attack Pearl Harbor. Yet differences of opinion as to exactly what was meant by "when necessary" persisted among Japan's leaders until late October. Tōjō, as prime minister, quickly felt the weight of his new office and wanted to proceed slowly. He insisted that more time be taken to study the situation. But General Gen Sugiyama and Admiral Osami Nagano, chiefs of the army and navy general staffs, respectively, wanted an immediate decision. A conference held in Tokyo on October 30 finally approved a program for continuing a diplomatic dialogue with the United States. This program later became known as Proposal A.

Proposal A, in brief, asserted that Japan would continue to observe all conditions of the Tripartite Pact; would not withdraw troops from either China or French Indochina (but would negotiate over China while keeping troops there for twenty-five years); and would not accept the Four Principles (set forth on April 16, 1941, by U.S. secretary of state Cordell Hull). The principles called for Japan to respect the rights and sovereignty of all nations; to not interfere in the internal affairs of other countries; to support the principle of equality, especially in trade; and to maintain the status quo in the Pacific. Japan did agree to the principle of equality in trading with China provided that the principle applied equally to the rest of the world.

On November 4, Foreign Minister Shigenori Togo dispatched a copy of Proposal A to Ambassador Admiral Kichisaburo Nomura in Washington, D.C. Togo added a note, part of which said (as decoded and translated by American code breakers and subsequently presented to U.S. secretary of state Cordell Hull):

> This time we are showing the limit of our friendship; this time we are making our last possible bargain, and I hope we can thus settle all our trouble with the United States peaceably.[33]

Before Nomura had time to digest the contents of Proposal A, Togo followed with Proposal B. The foreign minister instructed Nomura to present the second proposal as "a last effort" to negotiate, cautioning that its failure would drive the Pacific situation to "the brink of chaos."[34]

Nomura, a sincere man, enjoyed a pleasant relationship with Hull and had earned the secretary's respect. But Nomura's role in a diplomatic cat-and-mouse game forced him to become less than forthright in his dealings with the American. To act in devious ways contrary to his nature began to wear on Nomura, so much so that he offered to resign as ambassador. Only his loyalty to the emperor persuaded Nomura to continue to represent Japan in the critical negotiations with the United States.

The next day, November 5, Togo levied an even greater burden on Nomura by setting a deadline for the heretofore open-ended peace talks:

> Because of various circumstances, it is absolutely necessary that all arrangements for the signing of this agreement be completed by the 25th of this month. I realize that this is a difficult order, but under the circumstances it is an unavoidable one.[35]

The 25th was selected because *Kido Butai* was scheduled to leave Etorofu on November 26 (November 25, Washington time). If the United States accepted the latest Japanese offer before the fleet sailed, Japan would realize substantial savings in time, fuel, and personnel.

A Remarkable Prediction

When Nomura presented Proposal A to the U.S. secretary of state on November 7, Hull already knew the contents of Japan's latest diplomatic offering. Through the tireless efforts of American code breakers, the Japanese diplomatic code had been broken fifteen months earlier.

The Japanese did not believe that the Americans were smart enough to break their complex diplomatic cipher known as the Purple Code. But a team of U.S. Signal Intelligence Service (SIS) cryptanalysts

Lieutenant Colonel William F. Friedman (seen here in 1951) led the team of cryptanalysts that broke the Purple Code.

(code breakers) proved that it never pays to underestimate an enemy. Under the astute and untiring leadership of Lieutenant Colonel William F. Friedman, the Americans broke the Purple Code in August 1940, following eighteen months of exhaustive labor.

Japan's diplomatic service used several codes—the Purple Code and multiple versions of the so-called J code—to send messages from the foreign ministry in Tokyo to embassies and consulates overseas, including the consulate in Honolulu. From the summer of 1940 on, U.S. analysts were routinely intercepting and decoding Japanese diplomatic messages. By the fall of 1941, U.S. officials knew more about Japanese intentions than Ambassador Nomura did, for Tokyo gave Nomura his information on a need-to-know basis.

However, access to Japanese diplomatic codes did not reveal all of Tokyo's aims to U.S. officials. The Japanese army and navy initiated much of their government's strategies and policies, and the Americans had not yet broken Japan's naval codes. Thus Washington did not know of Yamamoto's plan to attack Pearl Harbor. But U.S. code breakers would crack that cipher too in a few months. The project dedicated to breaking the Japanese codes was aptly named "Magic." It follows that the analysts who performed such wizardry might reasonably be called "magicians."

These magicians armed Hull with foreknowledge of Nomura's diplomatic maneuverings. Hull remained cordial as always to the ambassador but dismissed the document (Proposal A) as containing nothing new. President Roosevelt agreed with Hull's assessment but instructed him to "strain every nerve to satisfy and keep on good relations."[36]

Admiral Harold R. Stark (left) wrote to Admiral Husband E. Kimmel (right) that the United States was "moving steadily toward a crisis in the Pacific."

On the afternoon of November 7, Hull attended a meeting of Roosevelt's cabinet. Apparently fearing the breakdown of diplomatic efforts to prevent war, Hull warned the president and other cabinet members of "the dangers of the international situation." Hull went on to brief them on Japan's latest proposal, stressing that in his view "relations were extremely critical and that we should be on the lookout for a military attack anywhere by Japan at any time."[37] Since the Japanese naval general staff and the Combined Fleet had just initiated their operational orders, Hull's warning displayed his remarkable grasp of the situation.

On that same day, as if to add an exclamation point to Hull's warning, Admiral Harold R. Stark, chief of naval operations, ended a letter to Admiral Husband E. Kim-

mel in Pearl Harbor with an even more remarkable prediction: "Things seem to be moving steadily toward a crisis in the Pacific. . . . A month may see, literally, most anything."[38] One month later fell precisely on the calendar date of December 7, 1941.

A SPECIAL ENVOY

In a November 15 message to Ambassador Nomura, Foreign Minister Togo expressed his gratitude for the ambassador's efforts and reaffirmed November 25 as the cutoff date for negotiations. Togo acknowledged Nomura's opinion that Japan should remain patient and wait to see what turn the war in Europe might take before committing itself to a war against the United States. But Japan could wait no longer. "The fate of the Empire hangs by a single thread," Togo declared, and exhorted Nomura to "please fight harder."[39] Togo's foreign ministry also sent instructions to the Japanese Embassy in Washington (and to other diplomatic missions) for destroying code machines in the event of an emergency.

That same day, Special Envoy Saburo Kurusu arrived in Washington from Tokyo, supposedly to assist Nomura in his ongoing negotiations. Japan's purpose in sending a special envoy to Washington at that time, other than to distract American officials from Japan's real intentions, remains a source of wonder. Nor is it clear how much, if anything, Kurusu knew about the Japanese plans for the next few weeks. Conceivably, Foreign Minister Togo sent Kurusu to Washington merely to ensure that Nomura would "fight harder."

GREW SENDS SECOND WARNING

On November 17, as Yamamoto and *Kido Butai* personnel in Hitokappu Bay (Etorofu) hoisted toasts to a Japanese success at Pearl Harbor, Ambassador Grew in Tokyo sent a second clear warning to U.S. secretary of state Cordell Hull:

> In emphasizing the need for guarding against sudden military or naval actions by Japan in areas not at present involved in the China conflict, I am taking into account as a possibility that the Japanese would exploit all available tactical advantages, including that of initiative and surprise. It is important, however, that our Government not (repeat not) place upon us . . . ma-

jor responsibility for giving prior warning . . . [as] our field of military and naval observation is almost literally restricted to what can be seen with our own eyes, which is negligible.[40]

POTENTIAL FOR A CONTINUING DIALOGUE

On that same day in Washington, D.C., Nomura introduced Kurusu to President Roosevelt and Secretary of State Hull. Kurusu, a veteran Japanese diplomat, had served earlier as Japan's chief negotiator of the Tripartite Pact. Hull's first impression of the small envoy wearing glasses and a neat mustache was one of immediate distrust. Hull wrote in his memoirs:

> Neither his appearance nor his attitude commanded confidence or respect. I felt from the start that he was deceitful. . . . His only recommendation in my eyes was that he spoke excellent English, having married his American secretary.[41]

(Left to right) Ambassador Nomura, Secretary of State Hull, and Special Envoy Kurusu.

That evening, Nomura and Kurusu paid an informal visit to Postmaster General Frank C. Walker. Although Walker served in no official diplomatic capacity, he took a keen interest in the peace negotiations. He and Nomura liked each other and shared a mutual respect. Each used the other as an unofficial sounding board for receiving and interpreting vibrations given off by the diplomatic maneuverings of their respective governments. On this occasion, Walker hinted to Nomura that a show of goodwill by Japan might aid the cause of peace. Walker said (as quoted by Nomura:

> The President is very desirous of an understanding between Japan and the United States. . . . If Japan would now do something real, such as evacuating French Indo-China [Vietnam], showing her peaceful intentions, the way would open up for us to furnish you with oil and it would probably lead to the re-establishment of normal trade relations. The Secretary of State cannot bring public opinion in line so long as you do not take some real and definite steps to reassure the Americans.[42]

Nomura acted quickly on Walker's hint, and he and Kurusu met with Hull the next morning (November 18). During a three-hour meeting, Nomura (without Tokyo's preapproval) conjectured, "If the Japanese were now to withdraw their troops from Indochina, could the United States ease their economic pressure to the point of sending small quantities of rice and oil?"[43]

Hull received Nomura's conjecture without enthusiasm, pointing out that troops withdrawn from Indochina might be redeployed in an equally unacceptable encroachment elsewhere. Nevertheless, the secretary, recognizing the potential for a continuing dialogue and thus a reasonable solution to their problems, promised to consider the Japanese proposal. But Tokyo, fearing that Nomura's independent proposal might delay or disrupt negotiations, rejected it and instead cabled Nomura to present Proposal B.

WEATHER REPORTS

On November 19, while Nomura and Kurusu prepared to present Proposal B in a meeting with Hull the next day, Tokyo dispatched to its Washington embassy (and its other embassies) instructions for interpreting the now-famous "Winds" messages, to be sent later. These instructions established a system for warning Japanese diplomatic posts of an imminent break in relations by including coded "weather reports" in the daily Japanese language shortwave news broadcasts and general intelligence broadcasts.

In short, to warn that Japanese relations were about to be severed with the United States, the weather forecast would be "east wind, rain"; with the USSR, "north wind, cloudy"; and with Great Britain, "west wind, clear."

The "Winds" instructions were intercepted and deciphered by U.S. code breakers. A continuous twenty-four-hour radio watch on the military listening networks was then initiated in anticipation of intercepting an "east wind" implementing message. Historians still dispute whether an implementing message was ever

U.S. code breakers deciphered the "Winds" instructions, designed to alert Japanese foreign embassies that diplomatic relations were about to cease.

broadcast by the Japanese or intercepted by the Americans. In either case, such a message would not have disclosed anything new to the Americans. Whether the "east wind, rain" message was ever broadcast or heard remains one of history's great intrigues.

HULL BUYS TIME

On November 20, Ambassador Nomura presented Proposal B to Secretary of State Hull. Stanley K. Hornbeck, adviser to the State Department for Far Eastern affairs, summarized the proposal as Japanese requests

that the United States agree to cease giving aid to China; that the U.S. desist from [increasing] its military force in the Pacific; that the United States help Japan obtain products of the Netherlands East Indies; that the United States undertake to resume commercial relations with Japan; that the United States undertake to supply Japan "a required quantity of oil"; while Japan on her part would be free to continue her military operation in and against China and to keep her troops in Indochina and to attack the Soviet Union, would have her funds unfrozen, would be able to buy with comparative freedom from the United States, would be assured adequate supplies of oil, and would be under no obligation to remove her troops from Indochina until she should have completed her conquest of China or there had been established "in the Pacific area" conditions of peace satisfactory to her.[44]

In Hull's assessment of the Japanese document, the Japanese proposal of November 20 was "of so preposterous [absurd] a character that no responsible American official could ever have dreamed of accepting [it]."[45] Yet he did not reject the proposal out of hand. He needed to buy time for the U.S. armed forces to shore up their defenses. And he needed time to prepare a counterproposal that might at last preserve peace.

ROOSEVELT'S MODUS VIVENDI

Japan's latest attempt to reach a peaceful agreement with the United States apparently impressed President Roosevelt more than it had Hull. After reviewing Proposal B, Roosevelt roughed out a modus vivendi, or compromise, of his own and sent it to Hull for formalizing. Roosevelt's pencil draft covered four principles to be acted on over the next six months:

1. U.S. to resume economic relations—some oil and rice now—more later.

2. Japan to send no more troops to Indochina or Manchurian border or any place South—(Dutch, Brit. or Siam [Thailand]).

3. Japan to agree not to invoke tripartite pact even if U.S. gets into European war.

4. U.S. to introduce Japs to Chinese to talk things over but U.S. to take no part in their conversations.

Later on Pacific agreements.[46]

Roosevelt's compromise offer represented a real hope for a peaceful solution to the problems between the two nations.

Kurusu, recognizing the importance still placed on the Tripartite Pact by the Americans, delivered a letter to the Department of State the next day. The letter declared that his government

> would never project the people of Japan into war at the behest of any foreign power: it will accept warfare only as the ultimate, inescapable necessity for the maintenance of its security and the preservation of national life against inactive justice.[47]

But Hull trusted neither Kurusu nor the government he represented. The next day, November 22, U.S. code breakers intercepted a message from Tokyo to Nomura, confirming Hull's suspicions. The message extended the deadline for negotiations to November 29 and warned, "THIS TIME WE MEAN IT, THAT THE DEADLINE ABSOLUTELY CANNOT BE CHANGED. AFTER THAT THINGS ARE AUTOMATICALLY GOING TO HAPPEN."[48]

That evening, Nomura and Kurusu called on Hull to urge a hasty reply to Proposal B. Hull replied with obvious irritation. "There is no reason why any demand should be made on us. I am quite disappointed that despite all my efforts you are still trying to railroad through your demand for our reply."[49] He did, however, promise a reply as soon as possible, intending to answer with a formalized version of Roosevelt's modus vivendi.

"THAT SOUTHERN MATTER"

On November 28, 1941, President Franklin D. Roosevelt met in Washington with his top civilian and military advisers. The president called the meeting to discuss the strategic implications of the recently sighted Japanese fleet heading toward Indochina. The key figures in attendance were the cabinet secretaries Hull, Knox, and Stimson, and the joint chiefs of staff Marshall and Stark. Secretary of War Stimson later recorded the following notes on that meeting in his diary (quoted in Prange, Goldstein, and Dillon, Pearl Harbor: The Verdict of History).

"It was the consensus that . . . an Expeditionary Force on the sea of about 25,000 Japanese troops aimed for a landing somewhere . . . changed the situation . . . [as to] whether or not we should address an ultimatum to Japan about moving the troops which she already had on land in Indo-China. It was now the opinion of everyone that if this expedition was allowed to get around the southern point of Indo-China and to get off and land in the Gulf of Siam, either at Bangkok or further west, it would be a terrific blow at all of the three Powers, Britain at Singapore, the Netherlands, and ourselves in the Philippines. It was the consensus of everybody that this must not be allowed."

Japan's latest move toward Indochina did little to encourage the success of diplomatic negotiations in Washington. In a telephone conversation with a Japanese foreign minister in Tokyo, Special Envoy Saburo Kurusu said, "As before [when Japan's move on Indochina in July 1941 triggered an economic freeze by the United States], that southern matter . . . was the monkey wrench."

A LESSON TO TEACH

On that same day (November 23 in Japan), the personnel of *Kido Butai* learned of their destination. They would leave in three days. Seaman Iki Kuramoto expressed the attitude that prevailed among his shipmates when he wrote:

An air attack on HAWAII! A dream come true. . . . What will the people at home think when they hear the news? Won't they be excited! I can see them clapping their hands and shouting for joy. These were our feelings. We would teach the arrogant Anglo-Saxon scoundrels a lesson.[50]

Meanwhile, peace negotiations continued in Washington.

THE HULL NOTE

On November 24, Hull met with representatives of Great Britain, China, Australia, and the Netherlands to review copies of Roosevelt's modus vivendi. China, with British support, expressed concerns that in the compromise America was "inclined to appease Japan at the expense of China."[51]

Secretary of War Henry L. Stimson called the president on the morning of November 26 to inform him that a Japanese fleet had been sighted sailing southward off Formosa (Taiwan). The fleet of some thirty to fifty vessels reportedly carried five divisions of combat troops. Upon hearing the news, Roosevelt "fairly blew up."

The president said that it

> changed the whole situation because it was evidence of bad faith on the part of the Japanese that while they were negotiating for an entire truce—an entire withdrawal [from China]—they would be sending this expedition down there to Indochina.[52]

Roosevelt then abandoned his proposed plan.

The secretary of state was left without a reply to Japan's Proposal B. Consequently, Hull and his staff hastily put together an answer for Nomura and Kurusu. The diplomatic note became known as the "Hull Note" or Ten Points. This long document basically restated the American position that had not varied in months.

Although the note was firm, Hull, in his diary entry of November 29, 1941, termed it a "broad-gauge, objective and statesmanlike document, offering Japan practically everything she has ostensibly been fighting for if she will simply stop her aggressive policy."[53] Nomura and Kurusu did not agree.

Tokyo interpreted Hull's note as an ultimatum. In turn, Washington perceived Tokyo's reaction to the note as a further indication of Japan's continuing refusal to negotiate in good faith. The threat of war loomed greater than ever on November 26.

WASHINGTON ALERTS PEARL HARBOR

On November 27, with the diplomatic picture growing grim in Washington, Army Chief of Staff George C. Marshall alerted his top commander in Pearl Harbor to the worsening situation. Marshall's War Department Message No. 472 to Lieutenant General Walter C. Short said:

> Negotiations with Japan appear to be terminated to all practical purposes with only the barest possibilities that the Japanese Government might come back and offer to continue. Japanese action unpredictable but hostile action possible at any moment. If hostilities cannot, repeat cannot, be avoided the United States desires that Japan commit the first overt act. This policy should not, repeat not, be construed as restricting you to a course of action that might jeopardize your defense. Prior to hostile Japanese action you are directed to undertake such reconnaissance and other measures as you deem necessary but these measures should be carried out so as not, repeat not, to alarm civil population or disclose intent. Report measures taken.[54]

Army Chief of Staff General George C. Marshall (left) instructed Lieutenant General Walter C. Short (right) to prepare for a Japanese attack.

Admiral Harold R. Stark, chief of naval operations, dispatched an even stronger message to Admiral Husband E. Kimmel, part of which follows:

> This despatch is to be considered a war warning. Negotiations with Japan looking toward stabilization of conditions in the Pacific have ceased and an aggressive move by Japan is expected within a few days. The number and equipment of Japanese troops and the organization of the naval task forces [indicate] an amphibious expedition against either the Philippines Thai or Kra Peninsula or possibly Borneo. Execute an appropriate defense deployment preparatory to carrying out the tasks assigned in WPL 46 [the navy's basic war plan]. Inform district and army authorities. A similar warning is being sent by the War Department.[55]

Following the receipt of these war warnings, a rash of misconceptions and miscommunications broke out among top army and navy commanders at Pearl Harbor. Much of the confusion resulted from a divided command in Hawaii and the failure of leaders of both services to understand their basic responsibilities. The army's basic mission was to defend Pearl Harbor and the Hawaiian Islands, whereas the navy's primary task was to deter Japanese aggression in the western Pacific. Their responsibilities often tended to overlap.

For example, the army was tasked to defend Pearl Harbor, but responsibility for long-range aerial reconnaissance fell to the navy. Conversely, the navy was not tasked to defend Pearl Harbor, yet the army mistakenly considered ships in port to form a part of the Hawaiian defenses. Misunderstandings, communication gaps, and the blurred lines of overlapping responsibilities resulted in a wanton lack of preparedness at Pearl Harbor—despite the clear warnings.

JAPAN'S MOUNTAINOUS TASK

On December 1, at five minutes after two o'clock in the afternoon, Premier Hideki Tōjō stood before Emperor Hirohito and a gathering of Japan's supreme civil and military leaders in Room One East of the Imperial Palace in Tokyo. With a grim face and grave voice, Tōjō told his listeners that Japan should not give in to American demands to vacate China and abort the Tripartite Pact. To do so, he warned, would be to threaten Japan's very existence. "Matters have reached the point where Japan must begin war with the United States, Great Britain and the Netherlands to preserve her Empire."[56] The prime minister proceeded to recount the long history of unsuccessful Japanese-American negotiations.

The ensuing spirited debate covered a range of problems—public morale, economic and financial considerations, national security, oil and raw materials, and other emergency precautions such as food supplies. Finally, war documents were signed by all present. Emperor Hirohito, in his private chambers, became the last to affix his signature, thus signifying his formal approval of Japan's decision to go to war.

At 1730 the next day, December 2, Admiral Isoroku Yamamoto dispatched a coded message to *Kido Butai*: "CLIMB MOUNT NIITAKA 1208".[57] Mount Niitaka, on Formosa, was the highest mountain in the Japanese empire, higher even than Mount Fuji. Philosophically, the message meant to "climb the highest mountain"; actually, it meant to proceed with the attack on Pearl Harbor on December 8 (Sunday, December 7, U.S. time). Yamamoto's message symbolized the mountainous task that lay before Japan. The defeat of the United States would be a long, steep climb. He could not yet anticipate the swift, dizzying descent on the far side of the mountain that would end in the defeat of his beloved homeland.

THE BURDEN SHIFTS

At 1130 on December 6, *Kido Butai* corrected course to 180 degrees due south toward Hawaii and advanced speed to 20 knots. Ten minutes later, Admiral Chuichi Nagumo ordered the historic Z flag hoisted on *Akagi*. It was the same flag that Admiral Tōgō had raised thirty-six years earlier during the Russo-Japanese War to signify the Japanese victory over the Russian czar's forces at Tsushima. *Akagi* then signaled a message from Yamamoto to encourage another great Japanese victory: "The rise and fall of the Empire depends upon this battle. Every man will do his duty."[58]

The warriors of *Kido Butai* filled the air with cheers. Far to the west, thousands of other Japanese warriors moved into posi-

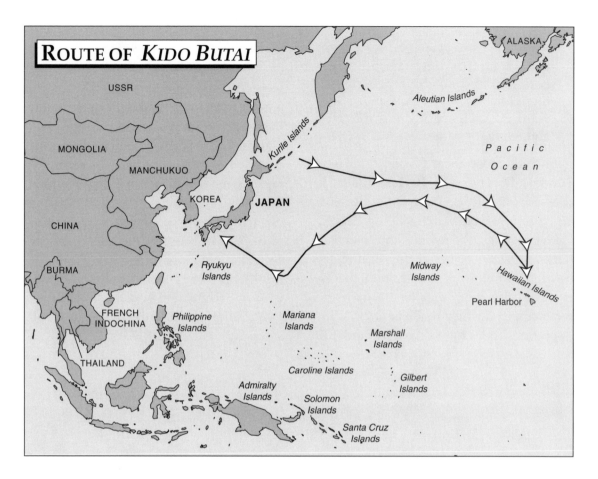

ROUTE OF *KIDO BUTAI*

tion and stood by in readiness to invade areas ranging from the Philippines to Singapore to the Dutch East Indies. Meanwhile, only hours before Admiral Yamamoto's X day, Japanese and American diplomats continued talking peace in Washington, D.C.

That night, Nagumo received some disappointing news. Ensign Takeo Yoshikawa, a spy who had been posing as a vice-consul at the Japanese consulate in Honolulu since April 1941, reported that no carriers were harbored in Pearl Harbor as of 1800 on December 6. (Admiral Kimmel had deployed the carriers *Enterprise* and *Lexington* at sea after receiving Stark's warning message.)

Among those most disappointed by the news were Commander Minoru Genda, the air operations officer, and Commander Mitsuo Fuchida, the designated leader of the air attack on Pearl Harbor. But as Fuchida wrote later:

Admiral Nagumo and his staff decided that there was now no other course left but to carry out the attack as planned. The U.S. battleships, though secondary to the carriers, were still considered an important target, and there was also a faint possibility that some of the American carriers might have returned to Pearl Harbor by the time our planes struck.

[The Japanese believed that four American carriers were based at Pearl Harbor at that time; actually, only *Lexington* and *Enterprise* were based there.] So the Task Force sped on toward its goal, every ship now tense and ready for battle.[59]

Fuchida arose aboard *Akagi* at 0500 on Sunday, December 7, 1941—X day. He dressed, carefully donning red underwear and a red shirt beneath his flying clothes. He had selected the red undergarments to hide any show of blood that might dishearten his followers. After joining his flyers in a celebratory breakfast of rice and red snapper, Fuchida made his way to the operations room for a sake toast and a final briefing. "On the blackboard was written the positions of ships in Pearl Harbor as of 0600 December 7," he recalled. "We were 230 miles due north of Oahu."[60]

Kido Butai had crossed more than three thousand miles of frigid, storm-tossed waters in the North Pacific without discovery. Just before daybreak, Nagumo's fleet reached its designated launch point. On *Akagi's* bridge, Admiral Nagumo turned to Commander Genda and quietly said, "I have brought the task force successfully to the point of attack. From now on the burden is on your shoulders and the rest of the flying group."

"Admiral, I am sure the airmen will succeed,"[61] Genda replied.

Chapter

4 *Tora! Tora! Tora!*

On December 7, 1941, under murky, predawn skies, explosive-charged catapults boomed simultaneously aboard the sister cruisers *Chikuma* and *Tone* at precisely 0530. Two single-engine, Type O reconnaissance seaplanes bolted skyward and winged off over the southern horizon. *Chikuma*'s plane proceeded toward Pearl Harbor, *Tone*'s toward Lahaina Roads. Their mission was to provide advance information to the first wave of attackers.

Commander Mitsuo Fuchida and his first-wave attack aircraft would not await the return of the reconnaissance planes. Their orders were to follow a half hour behind the seaplanes and receive the reconnaissance reports by radio while en route to target.

HOW THEY FELT

As *Kido Butai* steamed closer to Oahu and launch time drew near, Commander Kyozo Ohashi, senior staff officer of the Fifth Carrier Division, sat in *Shokaku*'s operations room, wondering what the next few hours would bring. He worried

about how his young, inexperienced pilots would perform in combat. Ohashi separated the feelings of his officers and flight crews into three classes:

> First, there were those who were virtually unmoved by the special mission of attacking Pearl Harbor, who considered the operation as their God-given duty, and who faced the immediate future with grim [indifference]. Into this class fell most of the older staff officers and key pilots.

Kaga (left) and Akagi *approach Hawaii on December 7, 1941.*

Secondly, there were those who thought the Pearl Harbor operation would succeed, but were apprehensive about the final outcome of the war. They wondered what was going to happen after the initial phase was over. Into this class fell the more intelligent of the younger officers who tried to look at things from a long-range viewpoint.

Finally, there were those who were nervous and afraid of what lay ahead. This class included the newer officers, the young trainees, and those of the crew who could only glimpse snatches of the overall plan.[62]

No one can predict the conduct of men in battle. Ohashi could only wait and hope that his pilots and crews would acquit themselves honorably and well.

NO TIME FOR CHANGES

By 0550, Nagumo's six carriers had drawn within 220 miles of Oahu. The admiral ordered them turned to the wind for launching aircraft. Captain Kiichi Hasegawa, *Akagi*'s skipper, spoke briefly to his assembled pilots. "All right, all the plans are made," he concluded, "let's get going!"[63]

Heavy swells showered flight decks with salt spray as the carriers turned eastward, pitching and heaving into a stiff wind. Flight decks tilted from 11 to 15 degrees. A 5-degree list was sufficient to cancel takeoffs under normal circumstances, but not today. The rough seas delayed takeoff twenty minutes.

A concerned Commander Shogo Masuda, *Akagi*'s air officer, greeted Fuchida at the carrier's command post on the upper flight deck. "What about this rough sea?" he asked. Both officers knew that there was no time to revise carefully laid plans.

"I have already given the word for action,"[64] Fuchida replied and, after saying his good-byes to those present, left to board his aircraft for the most important flight of his life.

A DATE WITH INFAMY

Prior to boarding his aircraft, each pilot readied himself for battle by tying around his head a *hachimaki* (a headband; the traditional symbol of a warrior's willingness

Commander Mitsuo Fuchida (seen here in 1950) led the air attack on Pearl Harbor.

"Zero" fighters (left) of the first wave are prepared for flight. A "Kate" torpedo bomber (right) makes its takeoff run.

to die) bearing the word *Hisso* ("certain victory"). The carrier's senior maintenance officer presented a specially made white *hachimaki* to Fuchida. As he handed it to Fuchida, the officer said, "This is a present from the maintenance crews. May I ask that you take it along to Pearl Harbor?"[65] The gift represented their desire to accompany Fuchida in spirit on his dangerous mission. Fuchida bowed and thanked him warmly, touched and humbled by the gesture from those whom he and his pilots depended on for so much. He wrapped the scarf securely over his helmet.

All six carriers launched in unison shortly after 0600. The fighters took off first. With a one-man crew and no bomb load, they required only a short run to become airborne. Lieutenant Commander Shigeharu Itaya led the sleek fighters off *Akagi*'s deck, dropping sharply to within fifteen feet of the sea. Lieutenant Seizo Ofuchi, acting as takeoff officer, held his breath. What an evil omen it would be if

the first plane to take off plunged into the sea. But Itaya's Zero lifted up and soared skyward, to the relief of all.

One hundred eighty-four aircraft followed. One fighter crashed on takeoff. Engine trouble forced a second fighter to stay behind. Fifty-one Aichi D3A "Val" dive-bombers; 40 Nakajima B5N "Kate" torpedo bombers; 49 horizontal bombers, also Kates (which served a dual role); and 43 Mitsubishi A6M "Zero" fighters made up Fuchida's first attack wave. Within a record time of fifteen minutes, 183 aircraft took to the air, formed up, and climbed above a cloud layer to an altitude of ten thousand feet. At about 0620, on Fuchida's signal, Japan's winged samurai turned toward Oahu and a date with infamy.

Blue Skies of Hawaii

Fuchida's air fleet was not the only group of aircraft heading toward Pearl Harbor

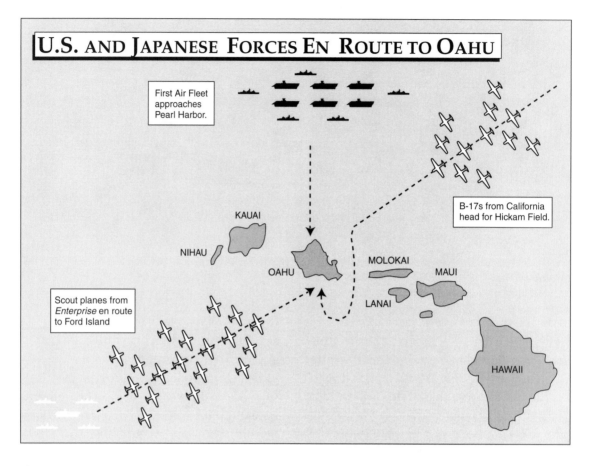

U.S. AND JAPANESE FORCES EN ROUTE TO OAHU

First Air Fleet approaches Pearl Harbor.

B-17s from California head for Hickam Field.

KAUAI

NIHAU

OAHU

MOLOKAI

MAUI

LANAI

Scout planes from *Enterprise* en route to Ford Island

HAWAII

that morning. At 0615, Vice Admiral William F. "Bull" Halsey had launched eighteen Douglas SBD Dauntless dive-bombers off the U.S. carrier *Enterprise*. The carrier, along with three heavy cruisers and nine destroyers, made up Halsey's Task Force Eight. Halsey had just delivered some marine aircraft to Wake Island and was homeward bound. He was due back in the Pearl Harbor channel at 0730, but rough waters had delayed refueling his destroyers. When dawn found him still two hundred miles from port, he drew a mix of SBDs from Scouting and Bombing Squadrons Six and sent them on ahead to scout the waters.

Two of the eighteen SBDs, led by Commander Howard L. Young, the *Enterprise* air group commander, sped off at once toward Pearl Harbor. Lieutenant Commander Bromfield Nichol, one of Halsey's aides, rode along as a passenger with Young. Because Task Force Eight was maintaining strict radio silence at sea, Nichol was to hand-carry Halsey's operations report to fleet commander in chief Kimmel. The remaining sixteen SBDs, led by Lieutenant Commander Halstead Hopping, formed up and followed Young's SBDs at 0637.

Meanwhile, approximately one hundred miles east of Oahu, the new day dawned behind a flight of twelve new Boeing B-17E bombers. Fresh from the factory, the American heavy bombers belonged to the Thirty-eighth and Eighty-eighth Reconnaissance Squadrons. Flying out of Hamilton Field, California, they were being ferried to Clarke Field, in the Philippines, under the command of Major Truman H. Landon. Landon's flight plan called for a refueling stopover at Hickam Field, adjacent to Pearl Harbor, with an estimated time of arrival set at 0800. Nearing the end of a long, fourteen-hour flight from the mainland, Landon's immediate concern was reaching Hickam before running out of gas.

Some two hundred miles to the north of Pearl Harbor, Admiral Nagumo ordered sixteen more reconnaissance planes aloft at 0630, four each from his battleships and heavy cruisers. Discovery by American ships or planes at this critical point might prove fatal to his fleet—and to the future of the Japanese empire.

The blue skies of Hawaii were about to become crowded.

FIRST BLOOD

While aircraft of both nations were still converging on Oahu, the twenty-five submarines of Vice Admiral Mitsumi Shimizu's Sixth Fleet had already fanned out into preassigned positions at the entrance to Pearl Harbor. The U.S. destroyer *Ward* was patrolling a two-mile square near the mouth of the harbor. At 0357, Lieutenant William W. Outerbridge, who had been *Ward*'s commander for only two days, received a blinker message from the minesweeper *Condor:* "Sighted submerged submarine on westerly course, speed nine knots."[66]

Outerbridge ordered general quarters (an alert for battle stations to be manned) and took up pursuit of the submarine. After an unsuccessful search, the new skipper secured from general quarters (called for the crew to retire from battle stations) at 0435. Lieutenant (j.g.) Oscar W. Goepner took over as officer of the deck.

At 0630, *Antares*, a stores and supply ship, spotted the same submarine trying to slip into the harbor through the antitorpedo netting, which had been opened earlier to admit two minesweepers. *Antares* blinked a warning signal to *Ward*. Goepner roused the captain, who again sounded general quarters. By then it was 0640.

Ward knifed full ahead through the water toward the sub and commenced firing within fifty yards of the intruder. The destroyer's first shot narrowly missed the submarine's conning tower, passing directly over it. *Ward*'s next round struck the submarine at the waterline, near where the conning tower joined the hull. The stricken vessel keeled over to starboard, slowed, and appeared to sink.

Lieutenant Outerbridge, leaving nothing to chance, shouted, "Drop depth charges!"[67] *Ward*'s whistle shrieked four times, as four depth charges set to explode at one hundred feet rolled off its stern. Outerbridge reported the submarine sunk at 0700. Some of Ward's crew feared that they might have sunk an American submarine by mistake. But their skipper felt confident that they had done the right thing.

Ship's Cook Third Class Dick Thill recalled, "We were later told that the lieutenant's call caused quite a stir among the Navy personnel back at Pearl, but it wasn't considered important enough to put the fleet on alert."[68]

Fifty-five minutes were still to elapse before 183 Japanese aircraft arrived over Oahu to strike with devastating fury from the air. Thus, oddly enough, American sailors, rather than Japanese airmen fired the first shot at Pearl Harbor. "And war being what it is," concluded Thill, "the *Ward* was sunk off the Philippines exactly three years to the day after the Pearl Harbor attack."[69]

CLOSING FAST ON TARGET

Shortly before 0700, Lieutenant Fusata Iida, leader of the Third Air Control Group (of Zeros), briefed his young pilots for the last time aboard *Soryu*. "What are you going to do in case you have engine trouble in flight?" he demanded, neither expecting nor wanting an answer. Without pausing, he provided his own answer. "In case of trouble I will fly directly to my objective and make a crash dive into an enemy target rather than make an emergency landing."[70] Such instructions left no doubt as to what was expected of them. And chance would allow several of them to so perform.

At 0705, Nagumo again ordered his carriers turned to the wind. The heavy seas had turned heavier, but nothing short of a typhoon at that point could stop Nagumo from launching his second attack wave. With visibility stretched to about twelve miles, the second attack wave began taking off at 0715 into a one-mile-high ceiling of cloudy skies. Again, the smaller, lighter fighters flew off first, with Lieutenant Saburo Shindo leading a group of thirty-six Zeros off *Akagi*. Fifty-four Kate horizontal bombers from *Shokaku* and *Zuikaku* followed, with overall commander of the second wave, Lieutenant Commander Shigekazu Shimazaki, in the lead. Last to launch were seventy-eight Val dive-bombers, the largest single group in the entire operation, commanded by Lieutenant Commander Takashige Egusa. One

Ward's gun crew poses with the gun that fired the first shot at Pearl Harbor.

dive-bomber aboard *Akagi* developed engine trouble and had to be scratched from the mission. All other aircraft took off without mishap. Launching of both the first and second waves had taken a total of ninety minutes.

Thirty-nine fighters remained behind to fly protective cover for *Kido Butai*, while 167 aircraft of the second wave sped off to the south. A combined force of 350 Japanese aircraft was now airborne and closing fast on target. It was now 0730.

NOTHING TO WORRY ABOUT

At the Opana mobile radar station, 230 feet above sea level near Oahu's northern Kahuku Point, army privates Joseph L. Lockard and George E. Elliot picked up a huge blip on their radar screen at 0702. They estimated that the blip represented fifty or more planes. The two privates reported their radar sighting to duty officer Lieutenant Kermit Tyler at Fort Shafter, thirty miles away: "There's a large number of planes coming in from the north, three degrees east!"[71]

Tyler mistakenly judged the blips to be the echoes of a flight of B-17s (Landon's) due to arrive from the United States. (Lockard and Elliot had erred by not reporting that the radar blip indicated fifty or more planes. Had they done so, Tyler could not have mistaken the sighting for Landon's B-17s. On the other hand, Tyler, for security reasons, had not mentioned the B-17s to Lockard and Elliot.) Tyler thought about it for a moment and said bluntly, "Don't worry about it."[72]

Japanese planes detected on radar were mistaken for American B-17s (pictured).

DELAYED DELIVERY

On the night of December 6, President Franklin D. Roosevelt had received the first part of a fourteen-part Purple Coded transmission that the code breakers had intercepted earlier. It contained a message from Japan's foreign ministry to be delivered to Secretary of State Cordell Hull at 1300 Eastern Standard Time (0730 Hawaiian Standard Time) the next day. The message clearly indicated Japan's intentions to forsake any further attempts to settle Japanese-American differences through diplomatic channels. It concluded:

> The Japanese Government regrets to have to notify hereby the American Government that in view of the

attitude of the American Government it cannot but consider that it is impossible to reach an agreement through further negotiations.[73]

After reading the message, Roosevelt turned to Harry Hopkins, his trusted adviser, and said, "This means war."[74] The ominous message indeed indicated that war was imminent, but it did not indicate where Japan might strike first. Or when. Existing records show beyond doubt, however, that Roosevelt and his advisers strongly believed that Japan would move first against Southeast Asia.

General Marshall, army chief of staff, cabled a warning to General Short in Hawaii just before noon the next morning (just before 0630 Hawaiian time):

> The Japanese are presenting at 1 P.M. Eastern Standard Time today what amounts to an ultimatum. Also they are under orders to destroy their code machine immediately. Just what significance the hour set may have we do not know but be on the alert accordingly.[75]

A series of unpredictable and inopportune events delayed delivery of Marshall's cable. Short did not receive the warning until long past the time for it to serve any useful purpose.

AMERICA'S SADDEST MORNING

The first attack wave droned steadily southward. Lieutenant Heita Matsumura, leader of *Hiryu*'s torpedo group, recalled viewing the splendor of the sun's arrival in the east:

The sunrise on that fateful morning looked similar to the Japanese naval flag.

> Soon the eastern sky brightened and each cloud ball was distinctly marked by bright side and shadow, sunbeams coming down through breaks in the clouds straight onto the blue sea. It was the suitable dawn for the epoch-making day, I felt at the time.[76]

The shafts of light seemed to form a giant replica of the Japanese naval flag. What better omen of a successful mission could be signaled by the gods of war?

Commander Fuchida also allowed himself to dwell briefly in the splendor of the scene and moment. He scanned the skies filled with the young eagles of Japan spread in perfect formation. How proud he felt to command them during his country's greatest undertaking. But the summons of great responsibilities could not be ignored for long. Commander Fuchida later recalled:

> At seven I figured that we should reach Oahu in less than an hour. But, flying over thick clouds, we could not see the surface of the water and had no check on our drift. I switched on the radio direction finder to tune in the Honolulu radio station and soon picked up some music. By turning the antenna I found the exact direction from which the broadcast was coming and corrected our course. We had been 5° off.
>
> Now I heard a Honolulu weather report: "Partly cloudy, with clouds mostly over the mountains. Visibility good. Wind north, ten knots."
>
> A more favorable situation could not have been imagined. About 7:30 the clouds broke, and a long white line of coast appeared. We were over the northern tip of Oahu. It was time for our deployment.[77]

At 0740, Fuchida found the skies over Oahu clear of American planes and antiaircraft fire. On a prearranged signal to his pilots, he shot off one flare to indicate that surprise had been achieved. This meant that the more vulnerable torpedo bombers would spearhead the attack. Two flares—the signal for an alert defense—would have called for the dive-bombers to strike first, thus diverting attention from the slower torpedo bombers. But the torpedo bombers failed to react to Fuchida's single flare. He waited ten seconds and fired a second flare.

The torpedo bombers, not having seen the first flare, deployed at once for attack. The dive-bombers had seen both flares, however, and rushed forward to strike the first blow. So much for well-laid plans.

In the resulting confusion, Fuchida had no choice except to follow the lead of his already committed aircraft. At 0749, he radioed to his planes *"To, To, To,"* the signal to attack (*to* being the first syllable of *totsugekiseyo,* "charge"). Four minutes later, Fuchida called out another signal: *"Tora! Tora! Tora!"* ("Tiger! Tiger! Tiger!")[78]—code words that notified the entire Japanese navy that his attack force had caught the Americans by complete surprise. Incredibly, his message stretched far across the Pacific and was received both in Tokyo and aboard Yamamoto's flagship *Nagato* in Hiroshima Bay.

A Japanese "Val" dive-bomber is seen here after releasing its weapon.

The air attack began simultaneously on Pearl Harbor, Fort Kamehameha, Schofield Barracks, and Ewa, Wheeler, and Hickam Fields at 0755. Sunday's calm turned to chaos in an instant. Diving aircraft screamed. Plunging bombs whined and exploded on targets with obscene sound and fury. Torpedoes streaked along whizzing paths across the heretofore still waters of Pearl Harbor, their lethal payloads directed against ships of steel and mortals of mere flesh, blood, and bones. Within minutes, billowing clouds of thick, black smoke from flaming metal climbed heavenward, in towering evidence of massive destruction.

So began the morning of America's greatest sorrow.

DEAD AIM ON FORD ISLAND AND BATTLESHIP ROW

Lieutenant Commander Shigeharu Murata, commanding forty Kate torpedo bombers,

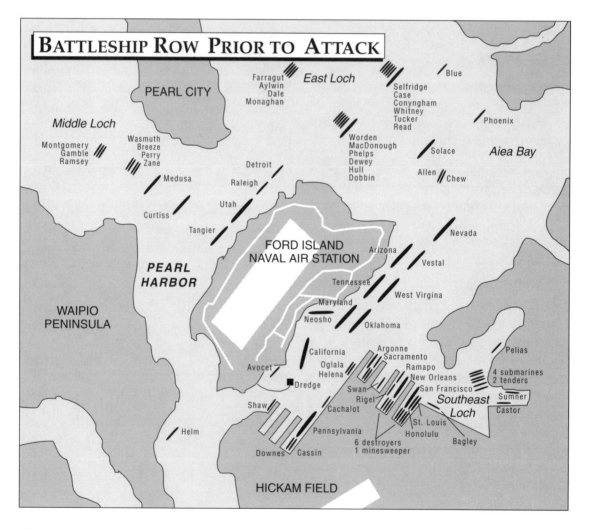

split his formation northwest of the marine base at Ewa. Two groups of eight Kates, under Lieutenants Tsuyoshi Nagai and Heita Matsumura, dove toward the west side of Pearl Harbor. And two groups of twelve Kates, led by Murata himself and Lieutenant Ichiro Kitajima, swung southeastward past Barbers Point, then circled Hickam Field in a wide north-northwestward arc before taking dead aim on Ford Island and Battleship Row.

Seven battleships—*Nevada, Arizona, Tennessee, West Virginia, Maryland, Oklahoma,* and *California*—lay moored alongside the southeast side of Ford Island. They formed the appropriately named Battleship Row and represented the bulk of American naval power in the Pacific.

On the opposite side of the island, torpedo bombers led by Nagai and Matsumura delivered the first blow against the fleet, scoring hits on the light cruiser *Raleigh* and the old battleship *Utah*. (By then, the ancient *Utah* was used only as a radio-controlled target ship.) Both ships began to list immediately. A third ship, the light cruiser *Detroit*, escaped unscathed.

Aboard *Raleigh*, Ensign John R. Beardall Jr., awakened by the concussion, rushed topside in his red pajamas. He had returned from liberty after midnight and was "not in the best of shape, but not the worst."[79] The ensign reached the quarterdeck just in time to see an airplane flash past. When the plane banked around to his left, he saw the big red balls painted on it and knew at once what was happening.

Caught still in his blue pajamas while reading the morning paper, Captain Robert B. Simons, *Raleigh*'s skipper, also scrambled above deck when he felt the concussion. He scrambled to the signal bridge and then climbed the ladder to the antiaircraft control station, where his gunners were just starting to fire. Simons shouted encouragement to his crew, then, after hurling a few expletives at the Japanese, returned to the signal bridge to direct the action.

Nagai, himself having overflown *Detroit*, continued across Ford Island and the channel separating the island from Dock 1010 and let fly with a torpedo aimed at the minelayer *Oglala*. As luck would have it, Nagai's torpedo streaked beneath the shallow-hulled minelayer and struck the light cruiser *Helena*, berthed inboard of *Oglala*. The blast rocked *Helena* and burst the seams of *Oglala*.

At the same time, Murata's Kates flew in single file at an altitude of only 132 to 165 feet, dropping as low as 66 feet over the southeast loch. Flying overhead protective cover, Lieutenant Yoshio Shiga, leader of the Second Air Control Group of fighters, watched the action below:

> They moved so slowly they looked like ants crawling along the ground. The U.S. Fleet in the harbor looked so beautiful . . . just like toys on a child's floor—something that should not be attacked at all.

But the torpedomen thought otherwise. Shiga remembered seeing "the splash in the water and a torpedo streaking for a battleship . . . just like a dragonfly laying an egg in the water."[80]

The "egg" was laid by Murata. Trailing Murata's three-plane element with

A Shocking Sight

"A Japanese plane had just struck a tree and caromed off the first tree and struck into a wall at my right at the ordnance machine gun shed. . . . The pilot was dead . . . stuffed in the tree, but the plane was on the ground, and the engine went around the ordnance shop. In caroming off [it] struck several men who were in the road. One man was completely decapitated. Another man apparently had been hit by the props, because his legs and arms and head were off, lying right on the grass."

The downed airplane was a Zero belonging to Lieutenant Commander Shigeru Itaya's first-wave fighter group.

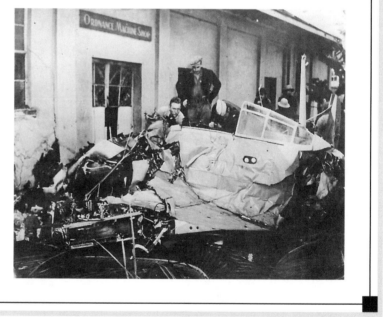

The wreckage of the shot-down Japanese Zero.

three planes of his own, Lieutenant Jinichi Goto saw Murata's torpedo strike the battleship *West Virginia*. Murata's other two planes also scored hits. *West Virginia* took a total of six torpedoes and began to list at once.

At the same time, Goto veered off to the left and directed his own pilots to nearby *Oklahoma*. Boring in low and slow, Goto concentrated on his speed, height, and correct release point. He recalled:

I was about twenty meters [sixty-six feet] above the water when I released my torpedo. As my plane climbed up after the torpedo was off, I saw that I was even lower than the crow's nest of the great battleship. My observer reported a huge waterspout springing up from the ship's location. *"Atarimashita!"* ["It struck!"] he cried. The other two planes in my group . . . also attacked *Oklahoma*.[81]

Their torpedoes scored the second and third of five hits on the hapless battlewagon.

FIVE MINUTES INTO THE ACTION

American gunners reacted quickly to the surprise attack on Pearl Harbor. First-attack-wave leader Fuchida later described the difficulties that he faced over Battleship Row at about 0800, only five minutes into the action:

As we closed in, enemy antiaircraft fire began to concentrate on us. Dark gray puffs burst all around. Most of them came from ships' batteries, but land batteries were also active. Suddenly my plane bounced as if struck by a club. When I looked back to see what had happened, my radioman said, "The fuselage is holed and the rudder wire damaged." We were fortunate that the plane was still under control, for it was imperative to fly a steady course as we approached the target. Now it was time for "Ready to release," and I concentrated my attention on the lead plane to note the instant his bomb was dropped. Suddenly a cloud came between the bomb sight and the target, and just as I was thinking that we had already overshot, the lead plane banked slightly and turned right toward Honolulu. We had missed the release

Plumes of smoke and geysers of water rise from damaged targets in this aerial photograph capturing the first minutes of the attack.

point because of the cloud and would have to try again.[82]

Fuchida's group circled around and on its second bombing run scored two hits on the battleship *Maryland.*

SMOKE AND FIRE ALL AROUND

When the Japanese aircraft struck along Battleship Row, Seaman Second Class Harlan C. Eisnaugle raced to his battle station aboard *Maryland.* From his station just below the bridge in the superstructure, he could see *Oklahoma,* already beginning to list. Seaman First Class Leslie Short, who had sought an isolated spot to address Christmas cards and write letters, was perched in his lofty machine-gun station in the mast when the attack began. He later recalled:

> Suddenly I noticed planes diving on the Naval Air Base nearby [on Ford Island]. At first I thought they were our planes just in a mock diving practice attack, but when I saw smoke and flames rising from a building, I looked closer and saw that they were not American planes. I broke out the ammunition nearby, loaded my machine gun and opened fire on two torpedo planes coming in from the east which had just dropped two torpedoes.[83]

Amid smoke and flames, Eisnaugle finally got his gun loaded and firing but could not determine whether his gun or others scored hits on the Japanese raiders.

A FEW BRIEF MOMENTS

A heartbeat after the first bomb fell on Ford Island, the Pearl Harbor signal tower telephoned Admiral Kimmel's headquarters and notified duty personnel of the attack. The duty staff relayed the message to the admiral's home in Makalapa Heights, overlooking the naval base.

Kimmel, who had just donned his white uniform, rushed outside and watched the planes begin to dive on the ships in the harbor. Mrs. Grace Earle, Kimmel's next-door neighbor, exclaimed, "There goes the *Arizona!*" The admiral watched in silence, but Mrs. Earle said later that "he looked stricken, and was as white as his uniform."[84]

At 0800, five minutes after the attack had begun, Kimmel radioed Washington, Admiral Stark, and all the forces at sea: "AIR RAID ON PEARL HARBOR. THIS IS NO DRILL."[85]

While Kimmel informed Washington and others of the Japanese attack, Commander Jesse L. Kenworthy, *Oklahoma's* executive officer and senior officer aboard, ordered his men to abandon ship. Recalled Kenworthy:

> As I reached the upper deck, I felt a very heavy shock and heard a loud explosion and the ship immediately began to list to port. Oil and water descended on the deck and by the time I had reached the boat deck, the shock of two more explosions on the port side was felt. As I attempted to get to the Conning Tower over decks

slippery with oil and water, I felt the shock of another very heavy explosion on the port side.[86]

He instructed the crew to leave over the starboard side, then calmly demonstrated the procedure. Quartermaster petty officer Stephen Bowers Young later wrote, "Kenworthy, immaculate in his dress whites, walked up the side and onto the bottom of the listing ship."[87] *Oklahoma* heeled over to port and capsized at 0805, sealing more than four hundred hands in an upside-down watery tomb.

Arizona took two torpedoes, one of which whizzed right under the shallow-hulled repair ship *Vestal*. From a vantage point behind *Oklahoma*'s antiroll keel, First Class Boatswain's Mate Howard C. French looked straight at *Arizona* and watched it explode:

There was an awful blast and a terrific concussion, but the force was upward

TORPEDO RUN

Chief Flight Petty Officer Juzo Mori, off the Soryu, *flew the second torpedo bomber in the attack led by Tsuyoshi Nagai. In* Zero! *by Masatake Okumiya and Jiro Horikoshi, with Martin Caidin, Mori tells the story of his torpedo run.*

"The assigned objectives of the *Soryu* torpedo bombers were the American battleships. . . . We dropped in for our attack at high speed and low altitude and, when I was almost in position to release my own torpedo, I realized that the enemy warship toward which I was headed was not a battleship at all, but a cruiser."

Mori circled his plane around for a second try. He recalled thinking,

"If I were going to die . . . I wanted to know that I had torpedoed at least an American battleship. . . .

Suddenly the battleship appeared to have leaped forward directly in front of my speeding plane; it towered ahead of the bomber like a great mountain peak.

Prepare for release. . . . Standby!

"Release torpedo!" . . .

The plane lurched back and faltered as antiaircraft [fire] struck the wings and fuselage; my head snapped back and I felt as though a heavy beam had struck against my head.

But . . . I've got it. A perfect release.

And the plane is still flying!"

instead of out. The foremast tilted forward, took a crazy angle and the ship went down immediately. I could see parts of bodies in the foremast rigging.[88]

Almost one thousand men died in that frightful explosion. It was 0810.

Berthed inboard, the more sheltered *Tennessee* and *Maryland* temporarily escaped serious damage, as did *Pennsylvania*, across the channel in dry dock one. But at the northern end of Battleship Row, *Nevada* had caught a torpedo on its port side at 0803. And at the southern end, *California*, flagship of the Pacific Fleet battle

DARK WATERS

Five minutes into the attack on Pearl Harbor, Japanese bombers scored multiple hits on the battleship Oklahoma, *and it began listing to port almost immediately. Young seaman Stephen B. Young, then assigned to the warship's number 4 turret, later recalled (in Nathan Miller's* War at Sea) *those first desperate moments when* Oklahoma *turned upside down.*

"Those of us who were left behind down in the powder handling room during those final seconds when the ship capsized were not aware at first that she was turning turtle. The darkness there was wild and confusing with objects of all descriptions being tumbled and thrown about. As we frantically fought to save ourselves, we became disoriented. . . . I felt the ship lurch. The deck slipped out from under me and my hands snatched at empty air. I was tossed and spun around, pitched into a great nothingness, suspended in air. . . . All of us—the living, dying and the dead—were whirled about. . . . Then the dark waters closed in over me as the ship came to rest—upside down on the bottom of the harbor. . . . I was surprised to find myself alive."

Oklahoma capsized to the left of Maryland.

Hit with two torpedoes and a bomb, the battleship Arizona *explodes, taking the lives of nearly a thousand men.*

force, had sustained two torpedo hits at 0805. Five minutes later, the flagship lost all power and began listing.

The torpedo attack lasted only a few brief moments. When it ended, the attackers had sunk or badly damaged five battleships, and had dealt crippling blows to two light cruisers, a minelayer, and a repair ship. The Kates left behind little doubt that their attack indeed had been "no drill."

5 A Unifying Crisis

At 0745, about a dozen Zeros rounded Hawaiiloa Hill and turned toward the nearby Kaneohe Naval Air Station. Three minutes later—and seven minutes before the Japanese air strike began at Pearl Harbor—Aviation Machinist's Mate Third Class Guy C. Avery heard "the sound of a lone plane quite near our house" at Kaneohe. The plane's engine sounded strange to him. He dashed to the window of the bungalow that he and a few squadron mates shared and looked out in time to see "Zeroes just beginning to fan out over the heart of the station and opening fire promiscuously." He yelled at once to his still-sleeping mates, "The Japs are here! It's war!" No one took him seriously.

One of his disbelieving mates replied, "Well, don't worry about it, Avery. It'll last only two weeks."[89]

KANEOHE NAVAL AIR STATION

Located on the eastern side of Oahu, Kaneohe was the home of Patrol Wing One, with a complement of thirty-six PBY-5 (Catalina) flying boats and a few miscellaneous aircraft. Four PBYs were moored in the bay that morning, spaced at intervals of about one thousand yards, according to Kaneohe's commanding officer, Commander Harold M. Martin. In observance of a sabotage warning issued the day before, most of the rest of the PBYs were parked on the seaplane ramp. Four were in number 1 hangar.

While enjoying Sunday morning coffee at his quarters, Martin saw the Zeros coming directly at him, flying at a height of about eight hundred feet. He assumed they were some of Halsey's planes coming in to land in advance of *Enterprise*. Martin took a closer look at them when his thirteen-year-old son David commented on their red circles.

Kaneohe's skipper pulled on his uniform over his blue silk pajamas and zoomed off in his car. By the time he arrived at his command post, one plane on the water was already burning. The Zeros were only getting started. Before leaving, the fighters destroyed all four PBYs moored in the bay.

At 0815, eighteen more Japanese planes, mostly dive-bombers (Vals), struck the field. The unprepared and underarmed Americans fought back, with little effect on the Japanese but well enough to make their commander proud. He commended their workmanlike performance under fire. Martin reserved a special word of praise for Mrs. Spencer, the post's civilian telephone operator, for her "calmness and initiative"[90] during the attack.

The second group of attackers devastated the air station, however, and a third group was still to come. Of Kaneohe's 36 PBYs, only 3 on patrol flights escaped without harm; 6 were damaged, and the remaining 27 were demolished.

BELLOWS FIELD

At Bellows Field nearby, American aircraft attempting to take off became easy prey for Japanese Zeros led by Lieutenant Fusata Iida. Base commander Lieutenant Colonel Leonard Weddington looked on in helpless frustration as two P-40s fell

Vice Admiral Halsey's SBD dive-bombers fly over Enterprise. *Commander Harold M. Martin thought that Japanese Zeros were Halsey's planes.*

This P-40 at Bellows Field was damaged on the ground. Other P-40s were destroyed as they attempted to take off.

victim to the Zeros. He afterward described their plight:

> I personally watched, wondering what would happen if the pilot [of the first P-40] was hit while taxiing, whether the airplane would just go on off, over the island, or whether he would die there, or whether he would groundloop, or what would happen. . . . Six different airplanes made passes at him and seemingly never hit him, but when he got on the runway and started to take off, they got right square behind him, and just as he got off, shot him down in flames; and he was turning, trying to give them a bad target, and crashed into the beach and burned there.
>
> The other one that they shot down taking off, I did not see take off, because there were some of them making passes at the position I was in at the time, and I ducked. I had seen him

taxiing down, however. They shot him down in the same manner, except that he was not so badly shot up, landed in the water about three-quarters of a mile to a mile down the beach, and swam ashore. He was not killed.[91]

Nine Japanese fighters demolished a Flying Fortress that had just landed on the runway. Several of Weddington's men removed the B-17's machine guns and started blasting away at the enemy fighters.

WHEELER FIELD

At Wheeler Field, in central Oahu—home of the Fourteenth Pursuit Wing—base commander Colonel William J. Flood had just opened the morning paper when he heard a fearful WHANG! and rushed outside in his pajamas. Japanese planes were bombing and strafing the base, targeting parked American planes, the officers' quarters, and even the golf course. Flood saw some of the Japanese pilots lean out of their cockpits and smile as they streaked by only a few feet off the ground. They flew so low that he could even see the gold glistening in their teeth. "Where're our fighters?"[92] he cried. The short answer was *all but demolished*.

The Fourteenth Pursuit Wing, commanded by Brigadier General Howard Davidson, held full responsibility for the island's entire aerial defense. There were 140 fighters in the wing: 87 fairly modern P-40s (35 of which were out of commission), 39 obsolete P-36s (20 of which where flyable), and 14 ancient P-26s (10 of which were flyable). The Forty-fourth and Forty-seventh Pursuit Squadrons were detached temporarily to nearby Bellows Field and Haleiwa Field to the north for gunnery practice. Most of the P-40s at Wheeler were lined up on the airstrip, wingtip to wingtip, to guard against potential sabotage attempts. Not one fighter made it aloft that morning.

Twenty-five Vals from *Zuikaku*, led by Lieutenant Akira Sakamoto, bombed Wheeler first at 0755. Two American machine gunners fired back valiantly, but without effect.

A wave of Lieutenant Kiyokuma Okajima's Fourth Air Control Group Zeros,

"THEY CAUGHT US WITH OUR PANTS DOWN"

Private Edward J. Gunger of the U.S. Army Air Corps woke up to the sound of cursing and low-flying aircraft at Hickam Field on Sunday morning, December 7, 1941. Years later, he described the ensuing action to Henry Berry (quoted in "This Is No Drill!") this way:

"I looked out the window and spotted the rising sun on the planes. They were flying so low you could see the faces of the pilots. . . .

That was it. My God, everyone is running around, bumping into each other. . . .

I made it to the planes and climbed in one of them. There was another airman already there. I helped him all I could to keep firing. I don't know if we hit anything or not, but at least we showed the Japanese we were there.

After the second wave had passed over, we looked around. What a mess! They had caught most of our planes on the ground. This was very important to their plan of attack. If we had been able to put a couple of hundred planes up in the air to meet them, we could have thrown a monkey wrench into their whole operation.

Well, we didn't. They caught us with our pants down and that's all there is to it."

off *Hiryu*, followed with a strafing attack. By the time fighter pilot First Petty Officer Kazuo Muranaka arrived, the entire field was ablaze.

The air over Wheeler Field was so crowded that Okajima and his Zeros soon departed for Ewa, the marine airfield west of Pearl Harbor. The Vals lingered at Wheeler long enough to demolish the hangars, post exchange, and enlisted men's barracks, killing several hundred instantly and seriously wounding many more. When the bombers left, one-half of Wheeler's fighters lay in smoking ruins.

HICKAM FIELD

A similar attack commenced on Hickam Field, just east of Pearl Harbor, at 0755. The headquarters of the Hawaiian Air Force resided at Hickam, as did the Eighteenth Bombardment Wing. The bomber wing's twelve B-17s, thirty-two B-18s, and thirteen A-20s represented the island's greatest threat for striking back against Nagumo's *Kido Butai*. Accordingly, the Japanese lashed Hickam with the full force of fighter, dive-bomber, and high-level bomber attacks.

The attack on Hickam Field destroyed many of the field's buildings, including this hangar. The damaged tail of a B-18 is visible at right.

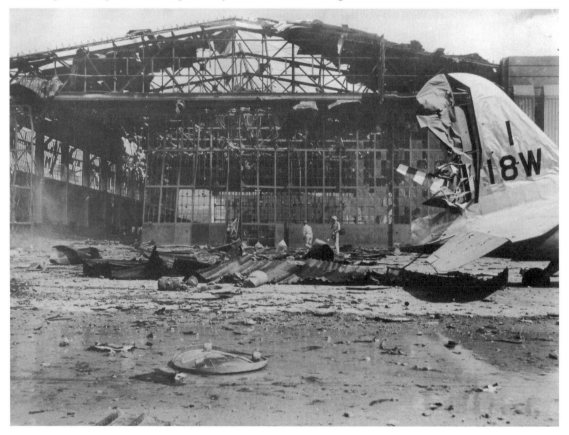

Lieutenant Robert Richard's wrecked B-17 at Bellows Field, where he made a forced landing while being attacked.

The first Japanese attack on Hickam came from two groups of dive-bombers from *Shokaku*, twenty-six in all, whose assigned mission was "to dive-bomb carriers in the harbor and, if they are not there, to attack Hickam air base" and then strafe until relieved by "friendly fighters." In the absence of any "carriers in the harbor," Lieutenant Iwakichi Mifuku and his squadron mates off *Shokaku* dive-bombed Hickam's hangars and "then strafed parked planes on the base."[93]

Twenty-four men were caught in the bombing and strafing attack while preparing several obsolescent B-18s for a training flight. Bomb blasts and machine-gun fire killed twenty-two and severed the legs off the other two.

Exploding bombs awakened Lieutenant Howard F. Cooper, commander of Headquarters Squadron, Seventeenth Air Base Group. He soon realized that dive-bombers were blasting the entire base and ripping the field to pieces.

Major Landon's twelve B-17s began arriving from the mainland at 0815, in the midst of flame and fury. A group of planes flew toward his formation from the south as if to greet him. Landon thought at first that they were friendly. Then they peeled over, revealing the bright red balls of the Rising Sun on their wings, and attacked his bombers with all guns blazing. Someone shouted over the intercom, "Damn it, those are Japs!"[94]

By some miracle, all twelve B-17s landed intact. Two landed at Haleiwa, one at Wheeler, another at Bellows, seven at Hickam, and the twelfth, pancaked down on Kahuku golf course. Once down, however, strafing fire destroyed one and badly damaged three others. But they had made it to their destination, albeit somewhat worse for the wear.

The Japanese attackers caught Hickam by complete surprise, just as they had surprised the fleet in Pearl Harbor. They knocked out more than half of the field's aircraft, trashed hangars, and destroyed many other important buildings. When the raiders finally turned away, they left behind 138 dead and missing Americans and 336 wounded. Of all the army bases, Hickam took the worst pounding that morning.

Kathleen Bruns Cooper, the nineteen-year-old daughter of a navy captain and newly married to a submarine officer, watched the attack on Hickam from her parents' neighborhood that overlooked the field. She recalled that the field looked "like a great sea of flame about a mile long." Cooper felt so outraged that she added, "If a Japanese pilot had walked in the house [right then], I would have tried to kill him."[95] No one doubted her.

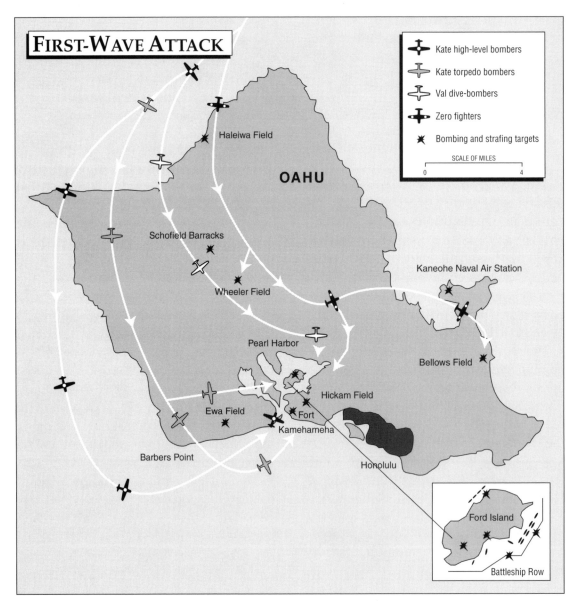

FIRST-WAVE ATTACK

Kate high-level bombers
Kate torpedo bombers
Val dive-bombers
Zero fighters
Bombing and strafing targets

SCALE OF MILES
0   4

Haleiwa Field

OAHU

Schofield Barracks

Kaneohe Naval Air Station

Wheeler Field

Pearl Harbor

Bellows Field

Hickam Field

Ewa Field

Fort Kamehameha

Barbers Point

Honolulu

Ford Island

Battleship Row

EWA FIELD

Across the bay from Hickam, twenty-one Japanese fighters roared around the Waianae Range northwest of Pearl Harbor and began shooting up the marine air station at Ewa Field at 0755. The Zeros made pass after pass. They flew as low as twenty feet off the ground, raking the personnel of Marine Aircraft Group Twenty-one (MAG-21) with incendiary, explosive, and armor-piercing rounds from 7.7-millimeter machine guns and 20-millimeter cannons. The Zeros concentrated their attack on the tactical aircraft lined up on the airstrip, destroying forty-seven of forty-eight fighter planes in the first fifteen minutes.

With their flyable aircraft rendered useless by the strafing attackers and without benefit of antiaircraft defenses, the marines answered the marauders with their only available means: rifles and .30-caliber machine guns stripped from wrecked planes. A few marines added Thompson submachine guns to the woeful mix.

After wiping out the marine fighters, the Zeros focused their attention on aircraft undergoing repair and personnel. A group of Vals joined the attack at 0835 and bombed hangars and other ground facilities. Twelve more Japanese planes struck Ewa for a third time between 0900 and 0930. But base and MAG-21 commander Lieutenant Colonel Claude A. Larkin described their final assault as "light and ineffectual."[96]

Of forty-eight planes lined up at Ewa Field on December 7, 1941, forty-seven never got off the ground. When the Japanese struck the marine air station that Sunday morning, Private First Class Bob Wells, USMC, and some comrades took cover in the walk-in refrigerators behind the mess hall. Wells later described what he saw right after emerging from the makeshift shelter:

> My God, what a sight! We had forty-eight planes of different types lined up. The Japanese had done a number on all of them.
>
> The two of us [Wells and another marine] each picked up bolt-action Springfield rifles. A jeep drove by with loaded bandoleers [ammunition belts] in it. A sergeant in the jeep was tossing out these bandoleers. We each caught one and went over to where they were building a new swimming pool. There was a bulldozer parked at the site. Using it for cover, we started shooting our rifles at the Japanese planes as they flew by. I don't think we hit anything, but we could let off some steam.
>
> Then, out of nowhere, two American planes appeared. I later found out they were piloted by two Army men named Welch and Taylor.
>
> Boy, did they tear into those Japanese planes! I saw two go down. There might have been more. . . .
>
> They [the Japanese] surely knocked the American airfields to pieces. Not only Ewa, but also Wheeler, Bellows, and Hickam. Just about every place we had planes was devastated.[97]

Zero pilot Lieutenant Yoshio Shiga would long remember his attack on the marine base. Years later he wrote:

> I was diving to take another run at Ewa. We had already bombed the hell out of the place. I saw this one American,

standing next to a disabled plane. He just stood there, firing and reloading his pistol. He didn't give an inch. He was truly a Yankee samurai.[98]

The "Yankee samurai" was marine Private First Class Mel Thompson, an angry sentry near Ewa's main gate, cranking off rounds from his .45. His act typified the fearless futility that American defenders displayed that morning.

HALEIWA FIELD

Only a handful of American fighter pilots made it off the ground to engage the enemy over Oahu that Sunday morning. Most notable among them were Second Lieutenants George S. Welch and Kenneth Taylor of the Forty-seventh Pursuit Squadron, temporarily assigned to Haleiwa Field on Oahu's northern shore. Except for one brief strafing pass on the tiny training field, the Japanese pilots had pretty much ignored Haleiwa in favor of choicer targets farther south. In the absence of the base commander and pilots standing by at Haleiwa on Sunday morning, the duty officer ordered a neat line of P-40s on the airstrip to be disbursed. Ignoring the duty officer's orders, Welch and Taylor boarded P-40s

Days after the attack, riflemen on Ford Island guard against further strikes by the Japanese. On December 7, American forces were caught completely by surprise.

Second Lieutenants Taylor (left) and Welch (right) earned distinguished service medals for shooting down seven Japanese planes. At far right, a Japanese dive-bomber goes down in flames.

and zoomed aloft at 0820. The two pilots promptly found themselves engaged, outnumbered, and fighting to stay alive.

Taylor described the action afterward:

> I made a nice turn out into them and got in a string of six or eight planes. I don't know how many there were. . . . I was on one's tail as we went over Waialua, firing at the one next to me, and there was one following firing at me, and I pulled out. I don't know what happened to the other plane. Lieutenant Welch, I think, shot the other man down.

Welch confirmed the kill. "We took off directly into them and shot some down. I shot down one right on Lieutenant Taylor's tail."[99]

The two lieutenants survived the uneven battle to refuel and return to action twice during the Japanese attack. By morning's end, the two pilots had shot down seven enemy planes between them. Welch was recommended for the Medal of Honor but received only the Distinguished Flying Cross because he had disobeyed orders.

At least a dozen fighter pilots from Haleiwa and Wheeler Fields made it into the air that morning, collectively accounting for ten confirmed kills and an undetermined number of probables. Two American pilots were killed in the course of these actions.

SCHOFIELD BARRACKS

In his acclaimed novel *From Here to Eternity*, writer James Jones described Japan's attack on Schofield Barracks in vivid detail. Jones based his fictional account on his own experiences as a company clerk in the Twenty-seventh Infantry Regiment. For the author, December 7, 1941, began much like any other Sunday:

At Schofield Barracks in the infantry quadrangles, those of us who were up were at breakfast. On Sunday morning in those days there was a bonus ration of a half-pint of milk, to go with your eggs or pancakes and syrup, also Sunday specials. Most of us were more concerned with getting and holding onto our half-pints of milk than with listening to the explosions that began rumbling up toward us from Wheeler Field two miles away. "They doing some blasting?" some old-timer said through a mouthful of pancakes. It was not till the first low-flying fighter came skidding, whammering low overhead with his MGs [machine guns] going that we ran outside, still clutching our half-pints of milk to keep them from being stolen, aware with a sudden sense of awe that we were seeing and acting in a genuine moment of history.[100]

The Ninety-eighth Coast Artillery Regiment was charged with the antiaircraft defense at Schofield Barracks, primarily an army infantry installation adjacent to Wheeler Field. Two soldiers assigned to communications duties with the regiment provided some antiaircraft defense of their own that morning, but not in the conventional manner.

At 0825, Lieutenant Stephen G. Saltzman heard what sounded like two planes with their throttles wide open "coming from the direction of Kole Kole." Then a low-flying Nakajima showed up. Saltzman described the action later:

Somewhere along the line I had grabbed a Springfield rifle. I didn't think the plane was going any more than seventy or eighty miles an hour. I emptied a clip (five rounds) into the plane. . . .

[Saltzman quickly reloaded.] Hell, I am an old duck hunter. I had a perfect shot at the pilot. I led the plane for an instant and let him have it. He just slumped over. The plane crashed in back of the schoolhouse. When the attack was over, we went over to see what I had brought down.

It wasn't a very pretty picture. . . . I should point out that my wire chief, Lowell Klatt, was also firing, but I know it was my shot that killed the pilot.[101]

Sergeant Lowell V. Klatt recalled that he and Saltzman ran to the crash scene and found two dead airmen. The Japanese had likely been killed on impact, because their badly burned bodies were crumpled down in the cockpit.

JAPANESE HERALD HEROIC DEEDS

While fortune favored most of Japan's airmen, the ten crew members of the Imperial Navy's five midget submarines—the Special Attack Unit—fared far less well. Their mission was to penetrate Pearl Harbor before dawn on December 7 and lie in wait on the ocean floor for the aerial attack to begin. When Nagumo's planes arrived overhead, the midget submarines would strike from below by torpedoing capital ships or the best targets available. The scenario did not play out that way.

The Americans sank four of the tiny submarines and captured the fifth. Not one midget submarine scored a hit at Pearl Harbor. The twenty-five large submarines fanned out south of the harbor entrance did little more than observe the action. (The submarine *I-70* was sunk in Hawaiian waters on December 10.)

Perhaps the most determined submariners were Ensign Kazuo Sakamaki and Petty Officer Second Class Kiyoshi Inagaki. Before leaving *I-24*, their parent submarine, they discovered a faulty compass on their midget craft. It would be impossible to reach their destination without a properly functioning compass. When asked by *I-24's*

captain what he wanted to do, Sakamaki replied, "Captain, I am going ahead." Inagaki seconded Sakamaki's decision. Then, caught up in the moment, both young men shouted, "On to Pearl Harbor!"[102]

But they ran afoul of reefs three times and failed to reach Pearl Harbor. Hung up on a reef for the third time, they tried to blow up their craft with an explosive charge and swim for shore. Inagaki drowned in the attempt, the charge failed to explode, and Sakamaki passed out from exhaustion and was washed ashore. When he revived, Sakamaki found himself in the

"KEEP 'EM FLYING"

Army nurse Blanche M. "Rusty" Kiernan experienced the devastating Japanese attack on Oahu while serving at Tripler Army Hospital. In a letter home, published in Litoff and Smith, We're in This War, Too, *Kiernan described some of the events a few days later.*

"We were visiting . . . at Hickam Field, Saturday night, December 6th. . . . They wanted us to stay all night but we didn't have permission so had to come home [to Tripler]. . . . The next morning a bomb landed in the street in front of their quarters and the house was riddled. . . . I don't know how they came out alive. . . . Our old quarters at Hickam had some glass blown out of the windows and a few holes in the roof and it was my day off too. We had just moved into Tripler in time. We had visited Sgt. Bonnie and his wife on Dec. 6th also and had a long chat. He was one of our neighbors and had been married only a month. . . . He was killed the next morning on his way to help out at the hangars. Also Lt. Richie who was PX [post exchange] officer and had called on us several times out there was killed as the PX was almost demolished. . . . There have been so many changes that I can't keep up with all of them. Many of the large schools have been turned into hospitals and quite a number of our nurses have been transferred to staff them. Please take good care of yourself and don't worry about anything.

I love you oodles and gobs, Keep 'Em Flying, Rusty."

custody of Sergeant David M. Akui. Sakamaki had just claimed the dubious honor of becoming the first prisoner captured by the United States in World War II. A bulldozer later towed his submarine ashore intact.

While being questioned, Sakamaki complained to his captors that his "honor as a soldier has fallen to the ground"[103] because he had allowed himself to be captured. He then pleaded for the Americans to kill him. They did not. Japanese accounts later chose to ignore Sakamaki's capture and instead heralded the heroic deeds of all midget submariners.

REACTIONS

While American casualties poured into the Pearl Harbor Navy Yard dispensary, and hospitals and temporary hospitals throughout the island, President Roo-

---

ANSWERING THE CALL

In "Remember Pearl Harbor" (published in the Reader's Digest Illustrated Story of World War II), Blake Clark, an associate professor of English at the University of Hawaii, recalls what it was like when the bombs fell on Oahu.

"We learned in Honolulu that Sunday how narrow the dividing line is between the soldier and civilian in wartime. Soon after the bombing started, a call came into the headquarters of the Hawaii Medical Association. The voice just said: 'Pearl Harbor! Ambulances! For God's sake, hurry!'

Within twenty minutes doctors and volunteer workers had stripped the insides of more than 100 delivery trucks of every description, equipped them neatly with previously prepared stretcher frames and were speeding to the scene of action.

Women of the Motor Corps, in every available car, were carrying men to Pearl Harbor. The three-lane highway was an inferno. Army trucks, official and unofficial emergency wagons, ambulances, Red Cross cars and hundreds of taxis rushing officers and men to their battle stations screamed up and down the six-mile road. The Motor Corps women were equal to the task.

The Army wounded were taken to Tripler Army Hospital. Surgeon [Colonel Edgar] King put in an emergency call for surgical teams to the doctors of Honolulu. Then occurred one of life's breathtaking coincidences. At that very moment, about fifty Honolulu doctors were listening to a lecture on war surgery delivered by Dr. John J. Moorhead of New York. The audience departed in a group for Tripler [Army Hospital]."

---

sevelt called Cordell Hull at 1405 that afternoon (0835 in Hawaii) to inform him of Admiral Kimmel's message about the Japanese attack. Officials in Washington still found it hard to believe that the Japanese would dare to attack Pearl Harbor.

Meanwhile, Ambassador Nomura and Special Envoy Kurusu had arrived at Hull's office and were waiting outside to deliver Tokyo's fourteen-part reply to American peace proposals. (Delivery of the diplomatic note, originally scheduled for 1300 on December 7, had been delayed because of the extra time required for decoding the lengthy document.) Roosevelt instructed Hull to receive the Japanese diplomats but not to mention anything about Pearl Harbor. The secretary was simply "to receive their reply formally and coolly bow them out."[104]

At 1420, Hull received them coolly and did not invite them to sit down. Nomura handed the secretary the note and apologized for not delivering it at 1:00 P.M. Hull asked sternly, "Why should it be handed to me at one P.M.?"

"I do not know the reason,"[105] Nomura answered honestly. Hull took delivery of the note but emphasized for the record that he was receiving the message at 2:00 P.M. He clearly wanted to etch the time in the minds of the Japanese diplomats.

The secretary of state scanned the document, then fixed an icy stare on Nomura and said:

> In all my fifty years of public service I have never seen a document that was more crowded with infamous false-

The captured Japanese midget submarine rests off the shore of Bellows Field.

hoods and distortions—infamous falsehoods and distortions on a scale so huge that I have never imagined until today that any government on this planet was capable of uttering them.[106]

Hull disallowed any response. He merely nodded toward the door. The two Japanese diplomats walked sullenly out of Hull's office with bowed heads.

Nomura added a brief entry to his diary later that day: "The report of our surprise attack against Hawaii reached my ears when I returned home from the state department; *this might have reached Hull's ears during our conversation.*"[107]

It had, of course, as Nomura learned later. The suddenness of Japan's attack both shocked and surprised the Japanese diplomat. Secretary of War Henry L. Stimson reacted somewhat differently. Upon hearing the news, his "first feeling was of relief that the indecision was over and a crisis had come in a way which would unite all our people."[108]

6 One Hour and Fifty Minutes

Lieutenant Commander Shigekazu Shimazaki's second attack wave—fifty-four Kate high-level bombers, seventy-seven Val dive-bombers, and thirty-six Zero fighters—arrived over Oahu at about 0840. Twenty-seven Kates were assigned to a second pass at Hickam Field; the remaining twenty-seven were to pound Ford Island again. All seventy-seven Vals were to concentrate on destroying as many ships as possible. In the meantime, the Zeros would sweep the air clear of enemy opposition and execute strafing attacks on Wheeler Field and Kaneohe.

When the original attackers exhausted their ordnance and turned northward to return to *Kido Butai*, their leader, Commander Mitsuo Fuchida, remained behind for a few minutes to direct the second-wave pilots. "Suddenly, at 0854," Fuchida wrote later, "I overheard Lieutenant Commander Shigekazu Shimazaki, flight commander of *Zuikaku* and commander of the second wave, ordering his 170 [sic] planes to the attack."[109]

The second wave would not enjoy the ideal attack conditions born of surprise and an unsuspecting enemy, as had the first wave about an hour earlier. Flame and smoke now shrouded targets and in-

terfered with bombing accuracy. And anti-aircraft fire laced the air with explosive puffs of flying steel. But the fate of Pearl Harbor and its surrounding military installations had already been decided. By then, American defenses had been rendered incapable of deterring the second-wave airmen from the efficient completion of their tasks. Hundreds of Americans would die trying, however, as a testament to Japanese treachery and American courage and determination.

MONAGHAN RAMS SUB

A moment before Shimazaki deployed his second wave, the U.S. destroyer *Monaghan* was cruising on a southwesterly course between Pearl City and Ford Island. Lieutenant Commander William P. Burford, *Monaghan's* skipper, had received orders from Fourteenth Naval District Headquarters to "contact *Ward* in defensive sea area."[110] Burford wanted to reach the open sea as soon as possible.

At 0839, a message from the seaplane tender *Curtiss* warned of a submarine sighting. Burford scoffed, refusing to believe that an enemy submarine of standard size could navigate in Pearl Harbor's shallow waters. Then a crew member pointed off the starboard bow and said, "Okay, Captain—then what is that dead ahead of us that looks like an over-and-under shotgun?"[111]

Burford looked off to the right about twelve hundred yards and spotted the "shotgun." (He was looking at the twin torpedo ports of a midget submarine.) Burford could not identify it, but he knew that it should not be there. He ordered full-ahead speed and set a course for ramming the undersea intruder. The next few minutes proved hectic for *Monaghan*'s skipper and his crew, as Burford noted afterward:

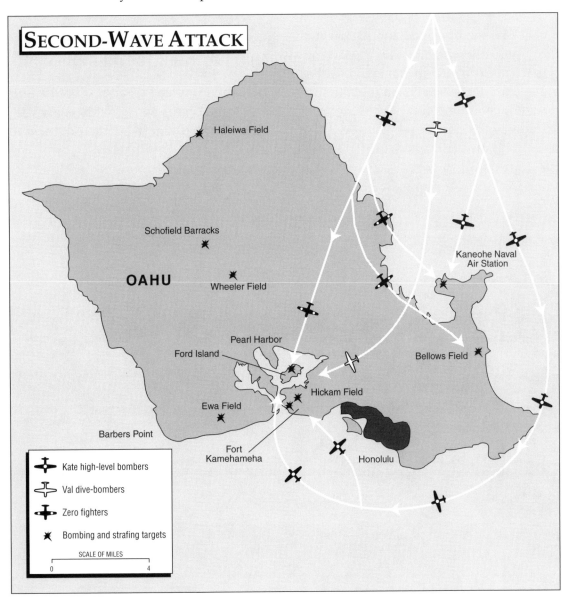

SECOND-WAVE ATTACK

Haleiwa Field

Schofield Barracks

OAHU

Wheeler Field

Kaneohe Naval Air Station

Pearl Harbor

Ford Island

Bellows Field

Hickam Field

Ewa Field

Barbers Point

Fort Kamehameha

Honolulu

Kate high-level bombers

Val dive-bombers

Zero fighters

Bombing and strafing targets

SCALE OF MILES

0   4

There was that sub coming directly at me, and I at him, and all that speed, and the firing by others, and a number of ships out ahead of me in restricted maneuvering space, and all the Japanese air attack behind us and our antiaircraft fire, their planes— God, a lot was going on in just a few minutes of time.[112]

At 0840, the damaged submarine surfaced and immediately took two direct hits from Curtiss's 5-inch and .50-caliber guns. The 5-inch shell penetrated the submarine's conning tower, shattering steel and killing the captain.

The small submarine fired two torpedoes at Monaghan and missed with both. The destroyer struck the submarine with a glancing blow and dumped two depth charges on it as Monaghan sliced on past. The charges ripped open the submarine's bow and it sank. Monaghan cleared the harbor safely at 0908.

KEEPING THE CHANNEL OPEN

Thirteen minutes earlier, just before Shimazaki's second-wave bombers arrived, Nevada got under way, despite severe

The midget submarine sunk by the Curtiss *and the* Monaghan *was later recovered and brought ashore by American salvage teams.*

torpedo and bomb damage incurred during the first attack. Lieutenant Commander Francis Thomas, the senior officer aboard *Nevada*, wanted to move the crippled battleship away from *Arizona*'s searing heat and flame.

Chief Quartermaster Robert Sedberry's steady hand guided *Nevada* through the narrow channel, past its burning neighbor, and on by the overturned *Oklahoma*. Sedberry threaded the bulky vessel through a narrow gap formed by the badly listing *Oglala* and the dredge *Turbine*. Moving smoothly toward the harbor mouth and the comparative safety of the open sea, *Nevada* flat ran out of luck.

Circling overhead, Commander Fuchida recognized a splendid opportunity to deal a double blow to the Pacific Fleet. If his airmen could sink *Nevada* at the entrance to the channel, the sunken vessel would bottle up the harbor and cancel Pearl Harbor's usefulness as a major operating base for perhaps months to come.

Nevada had just drawn abreast of the flaming floating dry dock, adjacent to Hospital Point, when a swarm of Egusa's dive-bombers struck at 0907. Five bombs exploded in *Nevada*'s superstructure and bow.

With his ship listing badly and still under attack, Thomas ordered Sedberry to run *Nevada* aground at Hospital Point at 0910. "From then on we were stationary, firing at every plane that came at us,"[113] recalled Seaman Second Class Dwight Cunningham years later. But the vital channel remained open.

GRACE UNDER PRESSURE

Lieutenant Commander Samuel G. Fuqua had pulled head-of-department duty aboard *Arizona* on December 6. As damage-control officer, he carried responsibility for the ship's watertight integrity and for keeping it afloat in case of battle damage. When *Arizona*'s forward ammunition magazine exploded at 0810 the next morning, killing Captain Franklin Van Valkenburgh, *Arizona*'s skipper, and Rear Admiral Isaac C. Kidd, First Battleship Division commander, Fuqua suddenly found himself senior officer in charge.

Just prior to the huge blast that killed more than a thousand men in one horrible instant, Fuqua and his damage-control crew had been fighting fires, trying "to keep the fire back by dipping water from the side in buckets and by the use of CO_2 extinguishers."[114] Following the blast, with the ship devastated beyond hope of saving it, he directed his efforts toward evacuating the wounded. For almost an hour, Fuqua stood fast in the face of machine-gun fire and advancing flame and searing heat, overseeing the removal of burned and mangled crew members.

By his own count, he personally evacuated more than seventy men. His devotion to ship and shipmates served as an inspiration to all the living still aboard and fighting for survival. Aviation Machinist's Mate Donald "Turkey" Graham spoke for many when he later said, "It seemed like the men painfully burned,

DIRECT HIT ON NEVADA

The battleship Nevada *tried valiantly to flee Pearl Harbor and escape to the open sea. But several Japanese bombs ended* Nevada's *flight in midchannel. Ensign John L. Landreth (in Prange, Goldstein, and Dillon,* December 7, 1941*) recalled near misses on the battlewagon and the "most noticeable" strike, which went through the gunfire director platform.*

"One plane came in and dropped one short. We could see that one go short and land in the water. Another one came in a little too far to the left and dropped it over us, and the third one came in right between these, and we could see before he did that it was going to be fairly close, and when he dropped it the bomb came right directly at our director, and we were certain it was going to hit us. It hit about a foot from the director and went through the director platform, went through the navigation bridge deck, went through the signal bridge and down into the captain's cabin and exploded somewhere probably below the captain's cabin, caused great damage in personnel in casement 4 and casement 6, just went below and was stopped by the third deck, armor deck."

Nevada *beached at Hospital Point, where it ran aground after taking five bombs.*

shocked and dazed, became inspired and took things in stride, seeing Mr. Fuqua, so unconcerned about the bombing and strafing."[115]

One of the last sailors to go over the side asked Fuqua if he too intended to swim to shore. "Not until the Japs leave,"[116] he replied. At about 0900, as nearly as Fuqua could later recall (although it was probably earlier), he reluctantly ordered abandon ship. His grace under pressure earned him the Medal of Honor and the undying gratitude of untold shipmates.

COURAGE KNOWS NO SIDES

Individual acts of valor occurred as regularly as heartbeats at Pearl Harbor. And, as keenly evidenced by the sacrifices of Lieutenants Fusata Iida and Mimori Suzuki, courage knew no sides.

Commencing at approximately 0900, Iida led nine Third Air Control Group fighters from *Soryu* in a third attack on Kaneohe Naval Air Station. He found the field already under attack by nine of Shimazaki's high-level bombers. One of their bombs had just struck a hangar with ammunition stores, igniting the ordnance and causing the greatest loss of life at the station. Iida's Zeros swept in from the east, across the distinctive line of cliffs behind Kaneohe known as the Pali, and started strafing everything that moved—and a lot that did not.

Iida's fighter was hit by ground fire and began streaming fuel as he climbed

After Arizona's *forward ammunition magazine exploded (pictured), Lieutenant Commander Samuel G. Fuqua led the valiant effort to evacuate the wounded.*

out of the field to rejoin his squadron mates. Signaling them northward to return to their carrier, he pointed first at himself and then at the ground. His pilots understood. Iida then turned back toward the field and plunged earthward, intent on keeping his vow to crash-dive into an enemy target rather than bail out. But the gallant pilot missed any important targets and crashed harmlessly into a hillside.

Three Japanese attacks on Kaneohe left the field in shambles, and all but three

---

FATAL PLUNGE

At Kaneohe Naval Air Station, Aviation Machinist's Mate Third Class Guy C. Avery witnessed Lieutenant Fusata Iida's fatal plunge into a nearby hillside. The Japanese fighter pilot had apparently honored an earlier vow to crash-dive into an American target should his Zero become disabled. Avery grimly recollected the end of Iida's story (in Prange, Goldstein, and Dillon, December 7, 1941).

"Lieutenant Iida's . . . body was taken up in a galvanized iron garbage can, not entirely out of disrespect—although heaven knows we despised him and his kind to the limit that day—but because we had no more suitable facility at hand. . . . The garbage can with its revolting contents was left on the front walk outside the sick bay entrance for the remainder of the day. We had sixteen of our own corpses awaiting care in the improvised morgue, and besides, there was nothing more that could be done for him then. Many of our own men were very indignant because he was given a dignified military funeral and interment along with those Americans who died that tragic day."

Lieutenant Fusata Iida's military funeral.

American aircraft were destroyed or severely damaged. The success of the attacks was blemished only by the loss of Iida and one other pilot who crashed into Kailua Bay. A third Japanese pilot crashed farther to the west at about the same time.

At 0905, antiaircraft fire from the seaplane tender *Curtiss*, the cruiser *Raleigh*, and probably other ships, struck Lieutenant Mimori Suzuki's Val during an attack on ships northwest of Ford Island. His Val, according to *Curtiss*'s log, "was hit badly and burst into flames." Suzuki then crashed—deliberately, according to observers—into *Curtiss*'s no. 1 crane, "where it burned completely."[117] Another vow kept.

Pennsylvania burns in the background with Downes at left foreground and Cassin at right.

THE LUCKY ONES

Somewhere around 0900, six SBDs from *Enterprise* arrived at Ewa, between attacks on the marine air base. "They came down in the normal method of identification and procedure and came to our field," according to base commander Larkin, "and we took them aboard."[118] He ordered them back in the air with all due haste. The SBDs proceeded from Ewa to Ford Island and received a hot welcome.

Ensign Cleo Dobson tried to land at Ford with what looked to him like every gun on the island shooting at him. He barely made it down through a storm of tracers and bursting pom-pom shells. Commanders Young and Nichol, bearing Admiral Halsey's message to Admiral Kimmel, experienced similar landing difficulties. Nichol recalled that they "went through the damnest amount of anti-aircraft fire and bullet fire he had ever seen, before or since, and finally got in to the field at Ford Island."[119]

This pair of SBD dive-bombers was among the lucky ones from *Enterprise*. Of eighteen scouts sent to Pearl Harbor in advance of Halsey's task force, five fell to Japanese Zeros or "friendly" antiaircraft fire.

INSPIRING WORDS

Luck deserted *Pennsylvania* when one of Egusa's dive-bombers discovered the battleship in dry dock one and scored a direct hit at 0902. Five minutes later, a high-level bomber landed another direct hit at the starboard side of the boat deck, killing two officers and eleven enlisted men. The blast also left thirty-eight wounded, fourteen missing, and two unidentified bodies.

Fire broke out on *Pennsylvania* and spread to two destroyers at the dock's head. They both had to be abandoned. By 0930, the fires had set off magazines and exploded torpedo warheads on the two destroyers. *Cassin* then rolled over against the stricken *Downes*, both vessels torn and gutted almost beyond recognition.

Three hundred yards west of *Pennsylvania*, the destroyer *Shaw* took three bomb hits between 0900 and 0930 while berthed with the tug *Sotoyomo* in the navy yard's floating dry dock two. Five more bombs struck the dock itself, setting it ablaze and ripping off its entire

After eight bombs struck Shaw, *the destroyer's forward ammunition magazine ignited and set off a huge explosion.*

bow. The flames spread out of control, igniting *Shaw*'s forward ammunition magazine and rocking the harbor with the most spectacular explosion of the morning. "I couldn't describe it," said an ensign who observed the blast from the repair ship *Vestal*. "It was just a great big whoof!"[120]

Another group of dive-bombers attacked *Curtiss* at 0912. Three bombs missed, but the fourth bomb struck the starboard side of the tender's boat deck, killing twenty-one crew members and demolishing everything within a thirty-foot radius of the blast. But *Curtiss*'s gunners fought back, firing at high-level bombers at 0928. Damage-control shipmates successfully struggled to save the ship.

Amid the smoke and flame, and under fierce and furious dive-bombing and machine-gunning attacks, the destroyers *Dale* and *Blue* managed to clear the harbor at 0907 and 0910, respectively, and thus survived to fight another day.

At 0912, a bomb struck twelve feet away from the ammunition ship *Pyro*; the ship was tied up at the ammunition depot in Pearl Harbor's remote West Loch. The bomb pierced the concrete and exploded beneath the pier. Although rocked by the blast, the fully loaded *Pyro* sustained only minor damage. This small miracle enabled a group of marines to transfer antiaircraft ammunition from *Pyro* to a small launch and distribute the much-needed ammo to various ships throughout the harbor.

At 0920, the old gunboat *Sacramento* sent a motor launch across the channel from 1010 Dock to help save the men aboard *Oklahoma* who were trapped alive in compartments rapidly filling with water. The gunboat moved twenty-seven men off the ship to safety, but rescue operations were just beginning. With their acetylene torches flared and sweating, oil- and smoke-blackened men worked desperately through the night to free their suffocating comrades. The last of thirty-two survivors would not see daylight until late the next afternoon, some thirty-six hours after *Oklahoma* had rolled over. Four hundred forty-eight men died aboard *Oklahoma* at Pearl Harbor.

Moored in 1010 Dock, about a quarter-mile south of dry dock one, the light cruiser *Honolulu* was attempting to get under way at 0925 when another group of dive-bombers bored in. Three bombs struck just forward of the light cruiser *St. Louis*, moored between *Honolulu* and the heavy cruiser *San Francisco*. Then a fourth bomb landed on the pier, about fifteen feet from *Honolulu*'s side. The blasts opened the cruiser's oil tanks to the sea and caused considerable flooding. *Honolulu* lost steam—and thus electrical power for lighting and electrically operated guns—and was condemned to remain in place. Its crew derived some solace, however, by shooting down one of the attackers.

Across the pier from *San Francisco*, much the same fate befell the heavy cruiser *New Orleans*, when something severed its power line to the dock. Despite disabled ammunition hoists, *New Orleans* was still a fighting ship. In the

A View from the Top

At about 0930 on December 7, Storekeeper Third Class Jack Rogo hurried from the Pearl Harbor infirmary to his official battle station on the roof of the Supply Department building, overlooking the navy yard. Twenty years later, he recalled that rooftop view (in Prange, Goldstein, and Dillon, December 7, 1941), forevermore etched in his memory.

"The panoramic view of Pearl Harbor was breathtaking. . . . To my right, across the channel was the USS *Shaw* all twisted in her dry dock. To my right on Ford Island lay the wreckage of our seaplane hangars with all of their windows blown out, and our seaplanes in a mass of twisted wreckage. Ahead of me the USS *Nevada*, listing, was steaming out to sea. She never made it and was beached at the mouth of the main channel. To my left was Battleship Row. I cannot remember the names or the positions of the ships now, but they were all damaged, listing, sunk, and some turned bottom up. Behind me, looking across Ford Island, I could see the bottom of the USS *Utah* rising from the water and the damaged fantail of the USS *Curtiss*."

A view of Battleship Row as seen from the Supply Department roof.

dark below decks, crew members formed a human conveyer belt to pass powder and shells topside to keep its guns firing.

While they worked, Chaplain Howard Forgy brought them apples and oranges and encouraging words. He apologized to the gun crews for being unable to hold church services that Sunday. Instead, he told them to "praise the Lord and pass the ammunition."[121] His words moved the men deeply and later inspired one of the most enduring and soul-stirring songs of World War II.

THE GREATEST WAR BEGINS

At 0944, the garbage barge *YG 17* and its stern crew braved fire and exploding shells to tie up alongside *West Virginia* and pour streams of water on the fires yet ablaze on the battleship. A minute later, the skies cleared. It was then 0945—one hour and fifty minutes after the first bomb had struck Ford Island.

The Japanese attack on Pearl Harbor had ended—and America's greatest war had begun.

Date of Infamy

Fuchida's first wave arrived back at *Kido Butai* at 1000. Fuchida himself, who had remained behind to direct the second wave, followed at 1200. Every Japanese aircraft capable of returning had done so by 1214. At 1315, Admiral Chuichi Nagumo ordered the withdrawal of *Kido Butai*. Nagumo's striking force, again under strict radio silence, turned homeward.

Amid the chaos and confusion that prevailed on Oahu that morning, the U.S. Navy managed only once to dis-cover the slightest clue as to the location of the Japanese fleet. When Nagumo broke radio silence to report to Tokyo at 1030, a navy radio technician intercepted the Japanese transmission signal. This enabled the technician to fix the signal at either a source bearing of 357 degrees, almost due north, or from the directly opposite bearing of 3 degrees. Extending its run of bad luck, the navy mistakenly interpreted the signal as originating from south of Oahu. As a result of this error, American search activ-

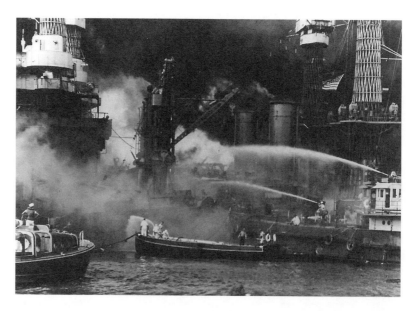

Firefighters extinguish the blaze aboard West Virginia *during the second wave of the attack. There were persistent rumors of a third wave.*

LIMITS

In his diary entry for December 9, 1941, Rear Admiral Matome Ugaki listed three reasons why (in his opinion) Admiral Isoroku Yamamoto chose not to override Admiral Chuichi Nagumo's decision not to risk a second attack (a third and possibly a fourth wave) against Pearl Harbor (excerpted from Prange, Goldstein, and Dillon, At Dawn We Slept).

"1. This time an approach could not be made without being detected. In consequence . . . our losses would be great although we could expect good results. There would be some chance, too, of our forces being flank attacked by enemy carrier planes; this might result in a pretty heavy blow to us. . . .

2. We haven't yet had a plan like that. It is not an easy task to draft a new plan and enforce it.

3. The most essential thing we have to consider right now is the mental factor involved. Who of those knowing the details of this operation from the beginning would dare to advocate strongly that we force another attack? What [Nagumo's officers and crew] did nearly reached the limit of their ability. To demand much more of them would only make them angry."

ities were concentrated in the south, while *Kido Butai* slipped away to the north.

THE ATTACK THAT NEVER CAME

Immediately after the last Japanese airplane cleared Oahu's skies, a wave of rumors surged across the island. The myth of a "third attack" (wave) pervaded both the military and civilian populations. In a report to Chief of Staff Marshall, General Short himself declared that the Japanese had struck Pearl Harbor for a third time on December 7 at 1130. On the basis of Short's dispatch, General Marshall reported to President Roosevelt, "Enemy Air Attack resumed 11:00 a.m., much less intense than former attack."[122]

Vivid accounts of the third attack (wave) appeared in rich detail in official army and navy reports, newspaper articles, and government memoranda. German Stuka dive-bombers were spotted, as were Japanese paratroopers. Japanese transports were sighted off Barbers Point. The threat of an imminent Japanese invasion spread across Oahu like pollen in a windstorm.

Secretary of the Navy Frank Knox flew to Oahu right away to assess the damages. Rumors were by then so deeply entrenched in the islands that Knox returned to the mainland convinced that there really had been a third attack (wave). On December 19, the secretary addressed the graduating class of the Naval Academy and reported:

> The third assault [wave] came two hours after the first one. With all the resources that were left to the same Army and Navy, we were ready, and that attack never got home. It encountered, as it approached Pearl Harbor, such a barrage from every gun and every ship that the enemy planes had to sheer off, and not a single torpedo found its mark or did the slightest damage to our ships or to our equipment ashore.[123]

An attack by a third wave never happened. Yet invasion rumors persisted for many days after the attack and would, in fact, become part of Hawaii's everyday life until the great American naval victory at Midway in June 1942. That victory curbed Japan's ability to launch an amphibious operation of that size.

Many survivors of the Pearl Harbor attack on December 7 might have welcomed another crack at the Japanese. Charley Hine, then serving at the naval hospital on Hospital Point, recalls:

> Here's what I remember best about the raid. On Saturday night we had four hundred beds full at the hospital. By Monday, all but six [who had just been operated on] of our original patients

Soldiers watch for enemy planes in a makeshift machine gun nest at Hickam Field. After the attack, Pearl Harbor prepared for the rumored third wave that never came.

had gone back to their ships. . . . Everyone wanted a crack at those Japanese.[124]

Thousands of Americans at Pearl Harbor shared that feeling on December 7. But the Japanese would not return to Oahu that day . . . or any other.

NAGUMO'S MISSED OPPORTUNITIES

Even today, more than a half-century after the event, more than a few military analysts and historians remain critical of Admiral Nagumo's failure to launch a second attack on Pearl Harbor when American defenses were in a state of total disarray. Many of those who took part in the first attack, including the attack leader Mitsuo Fuchida, favored a second attack. (The second attack urged by Fuchida and others should not be confused with the first and second waves of the first attack.) But Nagumo opted to stay strictly within the limits of his two mission objectives: to render the U.S. Pacific Fleet ineffective for at least six months and to return *Kido Butai* to Japan intact. He accomplished those objectives beyond his wildest imaginings.

In 110 minutes, the Japanese attackers had sunk five battleships—*Arizona, California, Nevada, Oklahoma,* and *West Virginia*—and seriously damaged three more—*Pennsylvania, Maryland,* and *Tennessee.* Also severely damaged were the light cruisers *Helena, Honolulu,* and *Raleigh* and the destroyers *Cassin, Downes, Helm,* and *Shaw.* The target ship *Utah* capsized, as did the minelayer *Oglala.* Four additional auxiliaries were

A destroyed B-17 at Hickam Field, one of the planes lost in the attack.

badly hit: the seaplane tender *Curtiss,* the tug *Sotoyomo,* the repair ship *Vestal,* and the floating dry dock two. The number of American vessels sunk or crippled totaled twenty-one.

American aircraft losses, both on the ground and in the air, numbered 165 planes.

Assessed damage to Oahu's military installations ran well into the millions of dollars, with damages to the Pearl Harbor navy yard alone estimated at $40 million (although that figure was probably inflated). But the greatest hurt came in American lives.

The total U.S. casualty figures recognized by most American authorities are 2,403 dead and 1,178 wounded. The majority of navy and marine deaths occurred on *Arizona,* while most army casualties were distributed among air

After the war, Masataka Chihaya, a former commander in the Imperial Japanese Navy (IJN), questioned why the IJN waged war on the United States. In his foreword to "An Intimate Look at the Japanese Navy" (reprinted in Goldstein and Dillon, The Pearl Harbor Papers), Chihaya writes, in part,

"The Japanese people are really mystified, because they know that the Japanese navy had always kept itself aloft of politics, domestic and international, devoting itself unswervingly to the business of the navy. No thought had been more foreign to it than to think and make itself an instrument of Imperialist policy.

Half a year has already passed since the armistice was signed on the *Missouri*, 2 September 1945. The signing was a historic scene. Since then, almost a year has just flown. No sign of the beginning of a revival from the exhaustion of war is yet in evidence. Debris all over the country greets our eyes. Then chaos and confusion. Not even assurance for tomorrow's food. We are far ahead of food! Not one single thing but reminds us vividly of defeat, defeat, defeat.

corps personnel at Hickam and Wheeler Fields.

Despite the widespread suffering and ruin left at Pearl Harbor by Japanese guns, bombs, and torpedoes, the situation could have been worse. For instance, the navy yard's oil reserves—a target even more vital than the warships—were not harmed. As Ken Creese, onetime seaman aboard the light cruiser *Detroit* and past president of the Pearl Harbor Survivors Association, points out:

> One of the biggest mistakes they made was in not hitting our fuel and oil reserves. Hell, with all the oil and gas we had, they could have set the whole island of Oahu ablaze.[125]

Even so, the Japanese attackers had all but demolished America's defensive stronghold in the Pacific. And they had done so at the amazingly low cost of twenty-nine aircraft: three fighters, one dive-bomber, and five torpedo planes in the first wave, and six fighters and fourteen dive-bombers in the second. Yet strategists continue to speculate about the implications of Admiral Nagumo's missed opportunities.

A DATE TO REMEMBER

Admiral Isoroku Yamamoto had demonstrated the enormous destructive force of a carrier-launched attack. Moreover, he had proved the carrier's superiority over the more conventional battleship. He had achieved a great but tainted victory. The U.S. Navy was down but not out and would meet Yamamoto again in six months at Midway.

In the interim, Americans would regroup and together set their minds to the task of winning an unwanted war. And they would long remember what happened at Pearl Harbor.

Shortly after noon on December 8, 1941, President Franklin D. Roosevelt addressed the Congress of the United States. In a solemn voice, he began, "Yesterday, December 7, 1941—a date that will live in

A poster showing a tattered flag at half mast commemorates Pearl Harbor and honors those who died in the assault.

infamy—the United States of America was suddenly and deliberately attacked by the naval and air forces of Japan."[126] Of all the important dates in American history, perhaps none is better remembered than this one.

The president pointed out that the surprise attack had been planned and carried out while Japan pretended to negotiate for peace. He assessed American losses and asked for American determination and resolve, while expressing confidence in American armed forces.

In conclusion, the president said, "I ask that the Congress declare that since the unprovoked and dastardly attack by Japan on Sunday, December 7, 1941, a state of war has existed between the United States and the Japanese Empire."[127] With but one dissenting voice in the House of Representatives, Congress did.

• • •

Long after World War II ended with Japan's unconditional surrender, Mitsuo Fuchida, who had led the aerial attack on Pearl Harbor, wrote, "The words 'REMEMBER PEARL HARBOR' became an oath that stirred up the fighting spirit of the American people. Successful though it was from the tactical point of view, the attack brought upon Japan a disgrace which did not vanish even after her defeat in the war."[128]

Notes

Introduction: Talking Peace and Planning War

1. Quoted in Trevor N. Dupuy, Curt John, and David L. Bongard, *The Harper Encyclopedia of Military Biography*. New York: Harper & Row, 1992, p. 586.

2. Quoted in David Bergamini, *Japan's Imperial Conspiracy*. New York: Pocket Books, 1972, pp. 241–42.

3. Quoted in Ronald H. Spector, *Eagle Against the Sun: The American War with Japan*. New York: Free Press, 1985, p. 40.

4. Quoted in Robert Leckie, *The Wars of America*, vol. 2. New York: HarperCollins, 1992, p. 726.

5. Quoted in John Costello, *The Pacific War 1941–1945*. New York: Quill, 1982, p. 71.

6. Quoted in Gordon W. Prange, with Donald M. Goldstein and Katherine V. Dillon, *At Dawn We Slept: The Untold Story of Pearl Harbor*. New York: McGraw-Hill, 1981, p. 167.

Chapter 1: Japan Decides on War

7. Quoted in John Toland, *Infamy: Pearl Harbor and Its Aftermath*. New York: Berkley Books, 1983, p. 260.

8. Quoted in Toland, *Infamy*, p. 261.

9. Quoted in Michael Slackman, *Target: Pearl Harbor*. Honolulu: University of Hawaii Press, 1990, p. 10.

10. Quoted in Toland, *Infamy*, p. 261.

11. Quoted in Slackman, *Target*, p. 10.

12. Quoted in Prange, Goldstein, and Dillon, *At Dawn We Slept*, pp. 10, 12.

13. Quoted in Clark G. Reynolds and the Editors of Time–Life Books, *The Carrier War*. Alexandria, VA: Time–Life Books, 1982, p. 41.

14. Winston Churchill, *Their Finest Hour*, vol. 2 of *The Second World War*. Boston: Houghton Mifflin, 1948, p. 544.

15. Quoted in Henry C. Clausen and Bruce Lee, *Pearl Harbor: Final Judgement*. New York: Crown, 1992, p. 75.

16. Quoted in Prange, Goldstein, and Dillon, *At Dawn We Slept*, p. 43.

17. Quoted in Prange, Goldstein, and Dillon, *At Dawn We Slept*, p. 204.

18. Quoted in Prange, Goldstein, and Dillon, *At Dawn We Slept*, p. 205.

19. Quoted in Slackman, *Target*, p. 14.

20. Quoted in Edward Jablonski, *Airwar*, vol. 1 Garden City, NY: Doubleday, 1971, p. 9.

21. Quoted in Jablonski, *Airwar*, p. 9.

Chapter 2: Under Way to Infamy

22. Quoted in Donald M. Goldstein and Katherine V. Dillon, eds., *The Pearl Harbor Papers: Inside the Japanese Plans*. New York: Brassey's, 1993, p. 6.

23. Quoted in Goldstein and Dillon, *The Pearl Harbor Papers*, p. 151.

24. Quoted in Prange, Goldstein, and Dillon, *At Dawn We Slept*, p. 300.

25. Quoted in Prange, Goldstein, and Dillon, *At Dawn We Slept*, p. 202.

26. Quoted in Prange, Goldstein, and Dillon, *At Dawn We Slept*, p. 203.

27. Quoted in Goldstein and Dillon, *The Pearl Harbor Papers*, pp. 146–47.

28. Quoted in Stephen E. Ambrose and C. L. Sulzberger, *American Heritage New History of World War II*. New York: Viking, 1997, p. 126.

29. Quoted in Costello, *The Pacific War 1941–1945*, p. 119.

Chapter 3: Point of Attack

30. Quoted in Costello, *The Pacific War 1941–1945*, pp. 116–17.

31. Quoted in Toland, *Infamy*, p. 263.

32. Quoted in Jablonski, *Airwar*, p. 9.

33. Quoted in Toland, *Infamy*, p. 170.

34. Quoted in Costello, *The Pacific War 1941–1945*, p. 116.

35. Quoted in Clausen and Lee, *Pearl Harbor*, p. 318.

36. Quoted in Costello, *The Pacific War 1941–1945*, p. 620.

37. Quoted in Prange, Goldstein, and Dillon, *At Dawn We Slept*, pp. 336–37.

38. Quoted in Prange, Goldstein, and Dillon, *At Dawn We Slept*, p. 337.

39. Quoted in Costello, *The Pacific War 1941–1945*, p. 621.

40. Quoted in Prange, Goldstein, and Dillon, *At Dawn We Slept*, p. 343.

41. Quoted in Toland, *Infamy*, p. 173.

42. Quoted in Goldstein and Dillon, *The Pearl Harbor Papers*, p. 177.

43. Quoted in Costello, *The Pacific War 1941–1945*, p. 622.

44. Quoted in Gordon W. Prange, with Donald M. Goldstein and Katherine V. Dillon, *Pearl Harbor: The Verdict of History*. New York: Penguin Books, 1991, p. 179.

45. Quoted in John Toland, *The Rising Sun*. New York: Random House, 1970, p. 175.

46. Quoted in Toland, *The Rising Sun*, p. 176.

47. Quoted in Toland, *The Rising Sun*, p. 177.

48. Quoted in Toland, *The Rising Sun*, p. 177.

49. Quoted in Toland, *The Rising Sun*, p. 178.

50. Quoted in Prange, Goldstein, and Dillon, *At Dawn We Slept*, p. 388.

51. Quoted in Toland, *The Rising Sun*, p. 178.

52. Quoted in Toland, *The Rising Sun*, p. 181.

53. Quoted in Prange, Goldstein, and Dillon, *Pearl Harbor*, p. 188.

54. Quoted in Slackman, *Target*, p. 58.

55. Quoted in Slackman, *Target*, p. 57.

56. Quoted in Costello, *The Pacific War 1941–1945*, p. 122.

57. Quoted in Nathan Miller, *War at Sea: A Naval History of World War II*. New York: Scribner, 1995, p. 200.

58. Quoted in Slackman, *Target*, p. 72.

59. Mitsuo Fuchida and Masatake Okumiya, *Midway: The Battle That Doomed Japan, The Japanese Navy's Story*. Annapolis, MD: Naval Institute Press, 1955, p. 50.

60. Quoted in Costello, *The Pacific War 1941–1945*, p. 130.

61. Quoted in Gordon W. Prange, with Donald M. Goldstein and Katherine V. Dillon, *December 7, 1941: The Day the Japanese Attacked Pearl Harbor*. New York: McGraw-Hill, 1988, p. 83.

Chapter 4: Tora! Tora! Tora!

62. Quoted in Prange, Goldstein, and Dillon, *December 7, 1941*, pp. 48–49.

63. Quoted in Slackman, *Target*, p. 72.

64. Quoted in Prange, Goldstein, and Dillon, *December 7, 1941*, p. 83.

65. Quoted in Walter Lord, *Day of Infamy*. New York: Bantam Books, 1991, p. 83.

66. Quoted in Lord, *Day of Infamy*, p. 27.

67. Quoted in John Toland, *But Not in Shame*. New York: New American Library of World Literature, 1961, p. 37.

68. Quoted in Henry Berry, *"This Is No Drill!"* New York: Berkley Books, 1992, p. 199.

69. Quoted in Berry, *"This Is No Drill!"* p. 200.

70. Quoted in Prange, Goldstein, and Dillon, *December 7, 1941*, p. 88.

71. Quoted in Toland, *But Not in Shame*, p. 38.

72. Quoted in Costello, *The Pacific War 1941–1945*, p. 133.

73. Quoted in Clausen and Lee, *Pearl Harbor*, p. 181.

74. Quoted in Clausen and Lee, *Pearl Harbor*, p. 80.

75. Quoted in Spector, *Eagle Against the Sun*, p. 95.

76. Quoted in Prange, Goldstein, and Dillon, *December 7, 1941*, p. 94.

77. Mitsuo Fuchida, "I Led the Attack on Pearl Harbor," in Reader's Digest Association, *Reader's Digest Illustrated Story of World War II*. Pleasantville, NY: Reader's Digest Association, 1978, p. 19.

78. Quoted in Slackman, *Target*, p. 76.

79. Quoted in Slackman, *Target*, p. 79.

80. Quoted in Prange, Goldstein, and Dillon, *December 7, 1941*, p. 115.

81. Quoted in Prange, Goldstein, and Dillon, *At Dawn We Slept*, p. 509.

82. Fuchida and Okumiya, *Midway*, pp. 52–53.

83. Quoted in Costello, *The Pacific War 1941–1945*, p. 135.

84. Quoted in Toland, *Infamy*, p. 11.

85. Quoted in Lord, *Day of Infamy*, p. 73.

86. Quoted in Costello, *The Pacific War 1941–1945*, p. 136.

87. Stephen Bowers Young, *Trapped at Pearl Harbor: Escape from Battleship* Oklahoma. New York: Dell, 1991, p. 82.

88. Quoted in Prange, Goldstein, and Dillon, *December 7, 1941*, pp. 140–41.

Chapter Five: A Unifying Crisis

89. Quoted in Prange, Goldstein, and Dillon, *At Dawn We Slept*, p. 519.

90. Quoted in Slackman, *Target*, p. 145.

91. Quoted in Prange, Goldstein, and Dillon, *December 7, 1941*, pp. 281–82.

92. Quoted in Toland, *But Not in Shame*, p. 43.

93. Quoted in Prange, Goldstein, and Dillon, *December 7, 1941*, p. 187.

94. Quoted in Toland, *The Rising Sun*, p. 274.

95. Quoted in Prange, Goldstein, and Dillon, *December 7, 1941*, pp. 192–93.

96. Quoted in Slackman, *Target*, p. 149.

97. Quoted in Berry, *"This Is No Drill!"*, pp. 192–93.

98. Quoted in Berry, *"This Is No Drill!"* p. 191.

99. Quoted in Prange, Goldstein, and Dillon, *At Dawn We Slept*, p. 534.

100. Quoted in Slackman, *Target*, p. 138.

101. Quoted in Berry, *"This Is No Drill!"* pp. 136, 137.

102. Quoted in Lord, *Day of Infamy*, p. 29.

103. Quoted in Slackman, *Target*, p. 227.

104. Quoted in Costello, *The Pacific War 1941–1945*, p. 138.

105. Quoted in Toland, *The Rising Sun*, p. 282.

106. Quoted in Ambrose and Sulzberger, *American Heritage New History of World War II*, p. 127.

107. Quoted in Prange, Goldstein, and Dillon, *At Dawn We Slept*, p. 554.

108. Quoted in Toland, *The Rising Sun*, p. 281.

Chapter 6: One Hour and Fifty Minutes

109. Fuchida and Okumiya, *Midway*, p. 54.

110. Quoted in Lord, *Day of Infamy*, p. 62.

111. Quoted in Lord, *Day of Infamy*, p. 125.

112. Quoted in Prange, Goldstein, and Dillon, *At Dawn We Slept*, p. 531.

113. Quoted in Berry, *"This Is No Drill!"* p. 233.

114. Quoted in Prange, Goldstein, and Dillon, *December 7, 1941*, p. 144.

115. Quoted in Slackman, *Target*, p. 121.

116. Quoted in Slackman, *Target*, p. 121.

117. Quoted in Prange, Goldstein, and Dillon, *December 7, 1941*, p. 261.

118. Quoted in Prange, Goldstein, and Dillon, *December 7, 1941*, p. 241.

119. Quoted in Prange, Goldstein, and Dillon, *At Dawn We Slept*, p. 520.

120. Quoted in Prange, Goldstein, and Dillon, *December 7, 1941*, p. 265.

121. Quoted in Lord, *Day of Infamy*, p. 146.

Epilogue: Date of Infamy

122. Quoted in Prange, Goldstein, and Dillon, *December 7, 1941*, p. 317.

123. Quoted in Prange, Goldstein, and Dillon, *December 7, 1941*, p. 317.

124. Quoted in Berry, *"This Is No Drill!"* p. 214.

125. Quoted in Berry, *"This Is No Drill!"* p. 130.

126. Quoted in Toland, *The Rising Sun*, p. 298.

127. Quoted in Toland, *The Rising Sun*, p. 298.

128. Quoted in Prange, Goldstein, and Dillon, *Pearl Harbor*, p. 493.

Appendix:
Wings of War

A6M: The Mitsubishi A6M "Zero" single-seat fighter and fighter-bomber was developed for the Japanese naval air force and first flown in April 1939. It was the only fighter plane used by the Japanese at Pearl Harbor and was superior to all American fighter planes at that time. It had a maximum speed of 332 miles per hour. Armament consisted of two 20-millimeter cannons and two 13.2-millimeter machine guns. The Zero was used throughout the Pacific Theater and became one of the most famous and most produced fighter planes of World War II. Evidence of the Zero's versatility could be seen in some models that were equipped with floats. Affixing pontoons to the fighter enabled the Zeros to be catapulted from the cruisers *Tone* and *Chikuma* and used to provide advance reconnaissance for Pearl Harbor attack waves.

A-20: The Douglas A-20 "Havoc" was a twin–engine attack bomber first flown in 1938. It was armed with nine .50-caliber machine guns and carried a two-thousand-pound bomb load. Its maximum speed was 332 miles per hour.

B5N: Used primarily as a torpedo bomber, the Nakajima B5N "Kate" also served as a dive-bomber. The Kate carried a crew of two or three at speeds of up to 225 miles per hour. It was armed with two 7.7-millimeter machine guns, one of which was mounted in the rear cockpit.

B-17: First flown in 1935, the Boeing B-17 "Flying Fortress" was a four-engine heavy bomber that was produced in several versions during World War II. Crew sizes varied from six to ten. The B-17 flew at speeds of up to 300 miles per hour. Its armament consisted of thirteen .50-caliber machine guns, and it carried a six-thousand-pound bomb load.

B-18: Developed in 1936, the Douglas B-18 "Bolo" was a twin-engine medium bomber that saw very limited service. Only 217 were made. Later versions equipped with radar were used for submarine patrols.

D3A: An awkward-looking, single-engine dive-bomber, with fixed landing gear, the Aichi "Val" became Japan's most effective bomber, sinking more Allied tonnage than any other bomber during the war. The Val was used most effectively at Pearl Harbor. It carried a crew of two at a top speed of 240 miles per hour. Armed with three 7.7-millimeter machine guns, it had an 813-pound bomb load capacity.

P-26: The Army Air Corps's first monoplane, all-metal production fighter, the Boeing P-26 "Peashooter" first flew in

1932 and entered service the following year. Obsolete before the start of World War II, the P-26 was slow (with a maximum speed of 234 miles per hour) and underarmed (with two .30-caliber machine guns, or one .30-caliber and one .50-caliber machine gun).

P-36: Developed for the Army Air Corps, the Curtiss "Hawk" was first flown in April 1936. The Hawk, a single-engine, single-seat fighter, was already outdated at the time of Pearl Harbor. It flew at speeds of 325 miles per hour and was armed with one .50-caliber and three .30–caliber machine guns.

P-40: A reworked P-36, the Curtiss P-40 "Tomahawk" represented the only relatively modern fighter in service when the Japanese struck Pearl Harbor. It had a top speed of 352 miles per hour and was armed with two .30-caliber and two .50-caliber machine guns. The Flying Tigers flew the Tomahawk with great success against the Zero in China during the first six months of the war.

SBD: Although conceived in 1938, the Douglas SBD "Dauntless" achieved distinction as the best dive-bomber design built by the American aircraft industry during World War II. The Dauntless carried a crew of two, flew at a maximum speed of 250 miles per hour, and had a maximum range of 1,345 miles. Armed with two .30-caliber and two .50-caliber machine guns, it could carry a twelve-hundred-pound bomb load.

Glossary

aft: Rear.

Atarimashita!: "It struck!"

Banzai!: Japanese battle cry; original meaning, "May you live forever!"

battlewagon: Battleship.

bearing: A compass direction.

bow: The extreme forward part of a ship.

Bushido: The code of conduct of the samurai of Japan, which embraces the virtues of courage, self-discipline, courtesy, gentleness, and honoring one's word.

China Incident: Japanese invasion of China; eight-year war between China and Japan commencing in 1937.

CinCUS: Commander in chief of the U.S. Fleet.

CinCPAC: Commander in chief of the U.S. Pacific Fleet.

CNO: Chief of naval operations.

conning tower: A raised structure on a submarine containing the periscope.

cryptanalyst: An expert in decoding coded messages; code breaker.

depth charge: An explosive device used against submarines, designed to detonate at a preset depth.

dive-bombing: A steep-dive (hell-diving) bombing approach.

embargo: A government order prohibiting the departure of commercial ships or goods from its ports.

emperor: The ruler of an empire, as Emperor Hirohito of Japan.

envoy: A person delegated to represent one government in its dealings with another.

fantail: Aft end of a ship.

flagship: A ship that carries an admiral and carries his flag.

flattop: Aircraft carrier.

forward: At or toward the front of a ship.

great all-out battle strategy: Japanese naval strategy based on luring the U.S. fleet—after first being weakened by Japanese submarine activity—into Japanese home waters for a massive, decisive sea battle for control of the Pacific Ocean.

greater East Asia coprosperity sphere: Japanese policy that called for the recognition of economic and political ties between Japan and several Southeast Asian nations.

grid location: A geographical location defined by an intersection of latitude and longitude lines on a map.

hachimaki: A headband worn by Japanese pilots.

hara-kiri: A ritual suicide by cutting out one's bowels, formerly practiced by Japanese officers when disgraced or under sentence of death; also spelled hari-kiri.

high-level bombing: A high-altitude, level-flight approach to deliver bombs on target.

Hisso: "Certain victory (message marked on *hachimaki*).

hull: The basic frame of a ship or aircraft.

intercept: Head off.

Kido Butai: Carrier striking force.

Kodo-Ha: The way of the emperor; a Japanese political movement that supported a totalitarian state controlled by the army.

League of Nations: Formed after World War I to prevent war and promote international cooperation; at one time the league comprised about sixty members.

logistics: Organization of military supplies and services.

MAG: Marine air group.

magazine: A store for arms and ammunition; a holder in or on a gun for cartridges to be fed into the gun chamber.

Manchukuo: The Japanese puppet state formed after the Japanese invasion of Manchuria in 1931.

Midway: An atoll located thirteen hundred miles west-northwest of Hawaii; the site of a great American naval victory over the Japanese during June 4–7, 1942.

militarist: One who advocates a policy of aggressive military preparedness.

modus vivendi: A workable arrangement or compromise.

Operation Hawaii: Japanese code name for the Pearl Harbor attack; later changed to Operation Z.

Operation Z: Japanese code name for the Pearl Harbor attack; earlier called Operation Hawaii.

ordnance: Military weapons, equipment, and ammunition.

Pearl Harbor: The U.S. naval installation at Oahu, Hawaii; headquarters of the U.S. Pacific Fleet.

perimeter: A line or strip bounding or protecting an area; outer limits.

port: Left side (of a ship).

radar: A system for detecting the presence, position, and movement, of objects by sending out short radio waves that are reflected by the objects.

reconnaissance: A preliminary search to gain information, especially for military purposes.

rendezvous: A meeting place.

Rengo Kantai: Combined Fleet.

sabotage: Willful damaging of materials or property or disruption of work by dissatisfied workers or hostile agents.

samurai: A military retainer of a Japanese *daimyo* practicing the warrior code of Bushido; the warrior upper class of Japan.

Senken Butai: Advance force.

shogun: One of a line of military governors ruling Japan until the revolution of 1867–1868.

Sino-: Chinese.

starboard: Right side (of a ship).

strategy: The plan for the entire operation of a war or campaign.

tactics: The art of placing or maneuvering forces skillfully in a battle.

"Tora! Tora! Tora!": "Tiger! Tiger! Tiger!" (message sent to Admiral Nagumo by Commander Fuchida to signify that the attack on Pearl Harbor was indeed a surprise).

torpedo bombing: A bombing technique that employs an extremely low and slow approach to deliver a torpedo on target.

totsugekiseyo: "Charge!" (*"To, To, To!"*)

Treaty of Kanagawa: Treaty opening Japan to Western trade, signed by American commodore Matthew C. Perry and Japanese shogun Iyesada in 1854.

Tripartite Pact: Formal agreement that established a military alliance between Germany, Italy, and Japan during World War II; the three nations became known as the Axis Powers, or the Axis.

USSR: Union of Soviet Socialist Republics; Soviet Union.

Washington Naval Conference: Disarmament conference (convened in Washington, D.C., during 1921–1922), which limited Japanese warship construction to three tons for each five tons built by the United States and Great Britain; that is, a 5-5-3 tonnage ratio.

waterline: The line along which the surface of water touches a ship's side.

X day: December 7, 1941 (December 8 in Japan); the Japanese equivalent of D day; the date on which a military operation is set to begin.

For Further Reading

Robert J. Casey, *Torpedo Junction: With the Pacific Fleet from Pearl Harbor to Midway*. New York: Bobbs-Merrill, 1942. A personal reminiscence of the first six months of the naval war in the Pacific by a noted war correspondent and author.

Winston S. Churchill, *The Grand Alliance*. Boston: Houghton Mifflin, 1950. Sir Winston's marvelous recounting of the Second World War from January 1941 through January 1942, featuring America's entry into the war.

Eugene Lyon, "America on the Brink of War," in *The Reader's Digest Illustrated Story of World War II*. Pleasantville, NY: Reader's Digest Association, 1969. A glimpse of one of the wildest, most colorful periods in American history.

Masatake Okumiya and Jiro Horikoshi, with Martin Caidin, *Zero!* New York: Ballantine Books, 1956. The story of Japan's air war in the Pacific by a Japanese commander of many of its sea-air battles and the designer of the famous fighter plane; includes insightful text on the Japanese view of the Pearl Harbor attack.

Zenji Orita with Joseph D. Harrington, *I-Boat Captain*. Canoga Park, CA: Major Books, 1978. A Japanese submarine captain writes about the undersea war in the Pacific, including a periscoped view of the submariner's role in the attack on Pearl Harbor.

Saburo Sakai with Martin Caidin and Fred Saito, *Samurai!* New York: Ballantine Books, 1957. A personal account of Japan's air war in the Pacific written by the greatest Japanese fighter pilot to survive the war; includes an interesting account of Japan's December 8 attack on the Philippines, executed simultaneously with the attack on Pearl Harbor.

William L. Shirer, *The Rise and Fall of the Third Reich: A History of Nazi Germany*. New York: Simon & Schuster, 1959. A history of Hitler's Reich by a highly regarded foreign correspondent and historian; contains valuable insight into the German-Italian-Japanese axis during World War II.

Donald J. Young, December 1941: *America's First 25 Days at War*. Missoula, MT: Pictorial Histories, 1992. A fascinating illustrated account of America's first twenty-five days at war in World War II.

Works Consulted

Stephen E. Ambrose and C. L. Sulzberger, *American Heritage New History of World War II.* New York: Viking, 1997. A masterful updating of the standard reference work.

David Bergamini, *Japan's Imperial Conspiracy.* New York: Pocket Books, 1972. A massive, controversial book that indicts Emperor Hirohito as a war criminal, written by a Rhodes scholar and former editor of *Life* magazine.

Henry Berry, *"This Is No Drill!"* New York: Berkley Books, 1992. An oral history told through the personal accounts of survivors of the attack on Pearl Harbor.

Winston Churchill, *Their Finest Hour.* Vol. 2 of *The Second World War.* Boston: Houghton Mifflin, 1948. Portrays England's early struggles during World War II.

Henry C. Clausen and Bruce Lee, *Pearl Harbor: Final Judgement.* New York: Crown, 1992. Clausen, a former special investigator for Secretary of War Henry L. Stimson, and Lee, an esteemed editor of military manuscripts, have written a book that provides accurate and irrefutable answers to all the unanswered questions surrounding Pearl Harbor.

John Costello, *The Pacific War 1941–1945.* New York: Quill, 1982. Complete one-volume account of the causes and conduct of the Pacific War.

R. Ernest Dupuy and Trevor N. Dupuy, *The Encyclopedia of Military History.* New York: Harper & Row, 1977. A monumental work on warfare by two noted historians; includes a keen analysis of events occurring before, during, and immediately after Japan's attack on Pearl Harbor.

Trevor N. Dupuy, Curt John, and David L. Bongard, *The Harper Encyclopedia of Military Biography.* New York: Harper & Row, 1992. The researcher's sourcebook for information about the lives of major figures in military history.

Robert B. Edgerton, *Warriors of the Rising Sun.* New York: W. W. Norton, 1997. A chronicle of the Japanese military's transformation from honorable "knights of Bushido" into men who massacred thousands during the Pacific War.

Mitsuo Fuchida and Masatake Okumiya, *Midway: The Battle That Doomed Japan, the Japanese Navy's Story.* Annapolis, MD: Naval Institute Press, 1955. An account of the pivotal battle as seen by two Japanese participants.

Donald M. Goldstein and Katherine V. Dillon, eds., *The Pearl Harbor Papers: Inside the Japanese Plans.* New York: Brassey's, 1993. An outstanding book that reveals original Japanese documents on Operation Hawaii, including secret plans, battle group histories, and the intimate letters and diaries of the key Japanese naval officers who planned, organized, and executed the attack on Pearl Harbor.

Edward Jablonski, *Airwar*. Vol. 1. Garden City, NY: Doubleday, 1971. A history of aerial warfare during World War II; contains an excellent chapter on the Pearl Harbor attack, including some fine photographs of the action.

Robert Leckie, *The Wars of America*. Vol. 2. New York: HarperCollins, 1992. A comprehensive narrative of American wars from 1900 to 1992.

Judy Barrett Litoff and David C. Smith, *We're in this War, Too: World War II Letters from American Women in Uniform*. New York: Oxford University Press, 1994. A comprehensive account of uniformed women in the war.

Walter Lord, *Day of Infamy*. New York: Bantam Books, 1991. A gripping, vivid re-creation of Japan's infamous sneak attack on Pearl Harbor on Sunday, December 7, 1941.

Nathan Miller, *War at Sea: A Naval History of World War II*. New York: Scribner, 1995. Captures the total naval war in the Pacific in one sweeping narrative.

Iain Parsons, ed., *The Encyclopedia of Air Warfare*. New York: Thomas Y. Crowell, 1974. A comprehensive study of aerial warfare, from the beginning of powered flight until 1974; includes a brief but excellent account of the Pearl Harbor attack.

Gordon W. Prange, with Donald M. Goldstein and Katherine V. Dillon, *At Dawn We Slept: The Untold Story of Pearl Harbor*. New York: McGraw-Hill, 1981. An authentic, absorbing account of Pearl Harbor from both the U.S. and the Japanese points of view; the masterwork on the event, its causes, and its aftermath by a historian who spent thirty-seven years preparing his book.

———, *December 7, 1941: The Day the Japanese Attacked Pearl Harbor*. New York: McGraw-Hill, 1988. A classic work that concentrates on the events that occurred immediately before, during, and after the Japanese attack on that long-remembered day.

———, *Pearl Harbor: The Verdict of History*. New York: Penguin Books, 1991. An exacting analysis of the underlying causes of Pearl Harbor, America's most disastrous military defeat.

Reader's Digest Association, *Reader's Digest Illustrated Story of World War II*. Pleasantville, NY: Reader's Digest Association, 1978. A collection of stories that together tell the tale of World War II.

Clark G. Reynolds and the Editors of Time–Life Books, *The Carrier War*. Alexandria, VA: Time–Life Books, 1982. A well-written and beautifully illustrated history of carrier warfare in World War II, including an excellent chapter on the Japanese attack on Pearl Harbor.

Michael Slackman, *Target: Pearl Harbor*. Honolulu: University of Hawaii Press, 1990. A fresh overview of the Pearl Harbor attack that uses contemporary documents and interviews with survivors to re-create the event and to examine its causes and the reasons for America's unpreparedness.

Ronald H. Spector, *Eagle Against the Sun: The American War with Japan*. New York: Free Press, 1985. A broad reassessment of U.S. and Japanese strategies during World War II, offering some provocative interpretations.

John Toland, *But Not in Shame*. New York: New American Library of World Literature, 1961. A remarkable history of the crucial first six months of the Pacific War, including a vivid depiction of the Pearl Harbor attack.

———, *Infamy: Pearl Harbor and Its Aftermath*. New York: Berkley Books, 1983. The noted historian's shocking and revealing account of Pearl Harbor's aftermath and the attempts to find scapegoats and cover up facts that might affix blame in high places.

———, *The Rising Sun*. New York: Random House, 1970. A narrative history of modern Japan from the invasion of Manchuria and China to the atom bomb; includes a fine account of the Pearl Harbor attack and the events leading up to it.

Stephen Bowers Young, *Trapped at Pearl Harbor: Escape from Battleship* Oklahoma. New York: Dell, 1991. The tragic tale of the more than four hundred men who died aboard *Oklahoma* and a handful of men who escaped entrapment aboard the capsized vessel, written by one who survived the ordeal.

Index

Wheeler Field, 42, 68, 78–81, 83, 85–86, 90, 106
Williamson, Kenneth, 23
"Winds" messages, 50–51
World War I, 13–14

X day, 30, 57–58

Yamamoto, Isoroku, 106–107
asks Genda to prepare attack plan, 25
considers dismissing Nagumo, 36
deploys submarines, 37
gives final instructions to Nagumo, 49
injured in Battle of Tsushima, 13
on Japanese resentment toward U.S., 14
on Japan's attacks on U.S., 21–22, 38
Operation Hawaii and, 23, 26–34
oversees rehearsal exercises, 40–41
sends message from *Akagi*, 56
supports Nagumo's decision to withdraw, 103
toasts success at Pearl Harbor, 49

Yankee samurai, 84
Yarnell, Harry E., 18–20
YG 17 (garbage barge), 101
Yoshikawa, Takeo, 57
Young, Bowers, 73
Young, Commander, 97
Young, Howard L., 62
Young, Stephen B., 74

Z flag, 56
Zero! (Okumiya and Horikoshi), 73
Zero fighter planes, 61, 64, 70, 76–80, 83, 90, 95–97
Zuikaku (carrier), 34, 41, 64, 79

Picture Credits

Cover photo: © Bettmann/Corbis

AP/Wide World Photos, 60, 64, 85 (left)

© Bettmann/Corbis, 11 (both), 31, 37, 47, 51, 92, 95, 96, 100

Brown Brothers, 27, 28, 43, 44, 48 (left), 49, 55 (left), 67, 70, 85 (right)

© Corbis, 30, 65, 71, 74, 75, 89, 107

Digital Stock, 97, 98

FPG International, 16

© Hulton-Deutsch Collection/Corbis, 23 (left)

Library of Congress, 77, 78, 81, 94, 102

© Museum of Flight/Corbis, 23 (right)

National Archives, 19, 26, 36, 48 (right), 55 (right), 61 (both), 80, 84, 104, 105

Naval Historical Center, Washington Naval Yard, 35 (both), 59

© Philadelphia Museum of Art/Corbis, 12

pixelpartners, 21

Martha Schierholz, 39, 42, 57, 62, 68, 82, 91

© Adam Woolfitt/Corbis, 66

About the Author

Earle Rice Jr. attended San Jose City College and Foothill College on the San Francisco peninsula after serving nine years with the U.S. Marine Corps.

He has authored more than thirty books for young adults, including fast-action fiction and adaptations of *Dracula*, *All Quiet on the Western Front*, and *The Grapes of Wrath*. Mr. Rice has written twenty books for Lucent, including *The Cuban Revolution*, *The Nuremberg Trials*, *The Final Solution*, *Nazi War Criminals*, *The Third Reich*, *Kamikazes*, and seven books in the popular "Great Battles" series. He has also written articles, short stories, and miscellaneous website materials, and has previously worked for several years as a technical writer.

Mr. Rice is a former senior design engineer in the aerospace industry who now devotes full-time to his writing. The author is a member of the Society of Children's Book Writers and Illustrators (SCBWI); the League of World War I Aviation Historians and its UK-based sister organization, Cross & Cockade International; the United States Naval Institute (USNI); and the Air Force Association (AFA). He lives in Julian, California, with his wife, daughter, two granddaughters, and two cats.